# *excellence in*
# Supplier
# Management

## *How to better manage contracts with suppliers and add value*

### *Best practices in Supplier Relationship Management and Supplier Development*

# *excellence in*
# Supplier Management

*How to better manage contracts with suppliers and add value*

*Best practices in Supplier Relationship Management and Supplier Development*

Stuart Emmett & Barry Crocker

ISBN 1-903-499-46-1
978-1-903499-46-7

Printed and bound in the United Kingdom by
4edge Ltd, 7a Eldon Way Industrial Estate, Hockley, Essex, SS5 4AD.

# Contents

# About this book

In writing this book, we have made best efforts not to include anything that, if used, would be injurious or cause financial loss to the user. The user is strongly recommended before applying or using any of the contents, to check and verify their own company policy/ requirements. No liability will be accepted by the authors or publishers for the use of any of the contents.

It can also happen in a lifetime of learning and meeting people, that the original source of an idea or information has been forgotten. If we have actually omitted in this book to give anyone credit they are due, we apologise and hope they will make contact so we can correct the omission in future editions.

This book parallels our earlier book *"Excellence in Procurement"* where our vision for Procurement was presented. Specifically related to suppliers this vision noted that:

- Procurement will not call suppliers vendors, as vendors are those who only seek to match the specification. Procurement will therefore recognise that suppliers are critically important in the provision of new ideas, innovation and value that can increase the performance of the organisation.
- Procurement will share with suppliers a joint common agenda to meet customer requirements. Procurement will recognise that its own organisations performance is indelibly connected to the performance of its suppliers.
- Procurement will be committed to its key suppliers for mutual benefit and gain over the medium to long term and will work together for continuous improvements year on year by having a joint restless search for inter-linked improvements.
- Procurement will ensure that "fit for purpose," supplier selection and evaluation is undertaken and that this key activity is not rule bound or covered by restrictive bureaucratic procedures that are now out of date.
- Procurement will recognise that the supply chain is a series of internal and external cross-functional processes and procurement will be an active and willing and leading member of the internal cross functional structure that connects to all of the external supply processes.

Unfortunately we are both of the opinion that many organisations, especially those serving internal customers, often fail or perhaps, stumble, in managing their suppliers. This is because the internal customer, or worse, someone else, is left to manage the selected suppliers, without perhaps realising that they have to!

Whilst this will be amplified further, suffice to note here that whilst the internal customer will often provide the kick-start to a procurement department (with the need and the specification), who then takes this over by sourcing a supplier and the eventual placing of the order/contract. After this, however, procurement departments so often "wave the order goodbye" and the internal customer is left without any conscious commitment to continue the procurement process cycle.

This is sub optimal; a classic example of a cross functional dependent process failing at the interfaces between departments.

There is therefore often little accepted practice of just how a procurement department relates to, or gets involved, with the essential supplier management in the procurement process. Whilst some departments fully do this, some other departments will just oversee the supplier management, whilst other procurement departments will ignore it.

We do not really wish to get into whose fault this is or who should be responsible, as such school ground politics simply serve to obscure the reality that suppliers will sit back and observe, wryly (and maybe to their advantage), the dynamics of such a sub optimal procurement processes.

This book therefore concentrates on highlighting the need for better supplier management and improving supplier management. It gives guidelines on how to better manage contracts and develop suppliers. The organisational responsibly for this is routed and determined by an organisations specific structure which in turn, is a policy matter for the strategic leaders of an individual organisations to determine. It cannot be systematically expected that supplier management is automatically going to be a procurement department role as there is just no "one-size-fits-all-model" for organisational structure.

We will cover all of these aspects in this book and we have arranged these in to the contents shown above. It should, however, be appreciated that to be effective and efficient in Supplier Management, we need to be looking at a joining up dependent processes. Therefore by dissecting processes into a fixed contents list, does present some inevitable overlaps and needed interconnections.

We will, above all else, be trying to answer the question "What kind of relationship do I need with suppliers so I can get the best from them, and therefore the best for me?" Meanwhile, the following diagram provides a simplified theme for this book; simply that suppliers and customers need connecting and that supplier management is the way to make this connection.

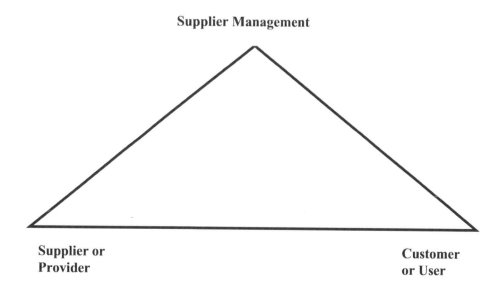

**Supplier Management**

**Supplier or Provider**

**Customer or User**

# About the Authors

## Stuart Emmett

My own journey to "today", whilst an individual one, does not happen, thankfully, without other peoples' involvement. I smile when I remember so many helpful people. So, to anyone who has ever had contact with me, please be assured you will have contributed to my own learning, growing and developing.

After spending over 30 years in commercial private sector service industries, working in the UK and in Nigeria, I then moved into Training. This was associated with the then Institute of Logistics and Distribution Management (now the Chartered Institute of Logistics and Transport).

After being a Director of Training for nine years, I choose to become a freelance independent mentor/coach, trainer and consultant. This built on my past operational and strategic experience, and my particular interest in the "people issues" of management processes.

Trading under the name of Learn and Change Limited, I now enjoy working all over the UK and on five other continents, principally in Africa and the Middle East, but also in the Far East and North and South America.
Additional to undertaking training, I also am involved with one to one coaching/mentoring, consulting, writing, assessing and examining for professional institutes' qualifications. This has included being Chief Examiner on the Graduate Diploma of the Chartered Institute of Procurement and Supply and as an external university examiner for an MSc in Procurement and Logistics.

My previous publications include, as co-author with Barry, *The Relationship Driven Supply Chain (2006)* and *Excellence in Procurement (2008)*. Other titles include, *Improving Learning & for Individuals & Organisations (2002)*, *Supply Chain in 90 minutes (2005)*, *Excellence in Warehouse Management (2005)*, *Logistics Freight Transport - national and international (2006)*, *Excellence in Inventory Management (2007)* (co-written with David Granville), *Excellence in Supply Chain Management (2008)*, and a series of seven *Business Improvement Toolkits (2008)* with individual titles on motivation, learning, personal development, customer service, communications, systems thinking and teams. Whilst these toolkits are written for a general audience, the case studies and examples have many supply chain applications.

I am married to the lovely Christine, and have two adult cute children, Jill and James; James is married to Mairead, who is also cute. We are additionally the proud grandparents of three girls (the totally gorgeous twins Megan and Molly and their younger sister, Niamh).

I can be contacted at stuart@learnandchange.com or by visiting www.learnandchange.com. I do welcome any comments.

## Barry Crocker

Barry is a lecturer in the Salford Business School at the University of Salford. He is currently Programme Leader for the MSc Procurement and Logistics and MSc Supply Chain Management. Previously, he has had many years industrial experience in various management positions in the field of transport, warehousing and physical distribution. He has been an assistant chief examiner for the professional stage of the CIPS Diploma.

His previous publications include, as co-author with Stuart, *The Relationship Driven Supply Chain (2006)*, *Excellence in Procurement (2008)* and *Procurement Principles and Management* by Bailey, Farmer, Crocker, Jessop and Jones (2008) 10th Edition.

Like Stuart, Barry has conducted many training sessions for multi-nationals in Africa, the Middle East and the Far East in the field of Logistics and Supply Chain Management.

# Foreword

I have known Barry Cocker and Stuart Emmett for a long time, and as a result I am aware of their tremendous passion both for this topic and for assisting others in learning about procurement and supply chain management related themes. Hence anything that they produce would be beneficial to those in the profession. That would be reason enough for reading this book. Yet there is much more here. The whole concept of supplier relationships, and more pertinently how to manage suppliers, has never been so much to the fore as it is now.

Procurement and supply chain management have gained recognition that was long overdue, as a strategic contributor to the competitive advantage of an organisation or, if in the public sector, then as a means of enabling economy, efficiency and effectiveness. To complement this awareness of the strategic contribution it is necessary to develop from processes and procedurally driven approaches into one that is about engagement with suppliers and enabling value creation from that relationship. This is a theme that needs to be understood by those seeking to understand and utilise the theory in a practical sense. Yet it is also about enabling those people who place contracts and are responsible for their progression to ultimate conclusion feel secure in the way that they managing the relationship in such a way as to gain value for their organisation

What this book does is to move from a broad understanding of procurement strategy including processes and procedures, with a recognition of the importance of the optimal selection of suppliers, to a consideration of the suppliers perspective of the activities discussed thus far. This allows a balanced view of supplier relationship management and subsequently a detailed insight into development of the supplier and ultimately management of the supplier. This is a book that is written unashamedly for those involved in, intending to become involved in or wishing to know more about the procurement perspective on how to manage suppliers. It utilises best practice to do so but is built upon the passion, knowledge and excellence of the authors. It is about joining up dependant processes and activities  to gain optimal benefit through procurement and supply chain management. It is seeking to bring customer and supplier together, through procurement and that is surely the future strategic role of procurement and supply chain management. It is a book of its time.

I highly recommend this book to you.

**Dr David M Moore**
**Director, Centre for Defence Acquisition,**
**Cranfield University,**
**Defence Academy of the United Kingdom**

# Part one: Procurement Strategy

## Suppliers and the supply chain

The Office of Government Commerce defines supply chain management as the "coordination of all parties involved in delivering the combination of inputs, outputs or outcomes that will meet a specified public sector requirement." (Source: *"Supply Chain Management in Public Sector Procurement - a Guide"*, Office of Government Commerce (OGC) June 2006).

Suppliers are a critical input in supply chain management, as the supply chain is the process which integrates, coordinates and controls the movement of goods, materials and information from a supplier, through to a customer and to the final consumer/user.

The essential point here is that the supply chain links all the activities between suppliers and customers to the consumer in a timely manner. Supply chains, therefore, involve the activities of buying/procurement, making/manufacturing, moving/distributing, and selling/marketing. The supply chain "takes care of business", following from the initial customer/consumer/user demand. Nothing happens with supply until there is demand represented by an order; it is the order that drives the whole process. Indeed some people (logically) argue that the term supply chain could be called the demand chain.

So, the supply chain bridges the gap between the fundamental core business aspects of Supply & Demand, as shown below:

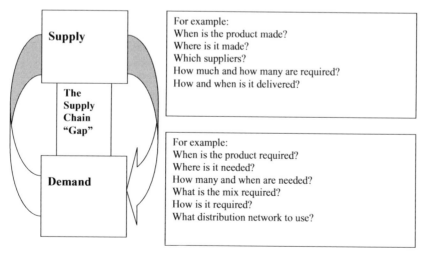

The philosophy of supply chain management is, therefore, to view all these processes as being related holistically so that they:

- Integrate, co-ordinate and control.
- the movement of materials, inventory and information.

- from suppliers through a company to meet all the customer(s) and the ultimate consumer/user requirements.
- in a timely manner.

A diagrammatic view follows, where it can be seen that the flow of products and the flow of information are represented by ideas, order creation, and cash/orders:

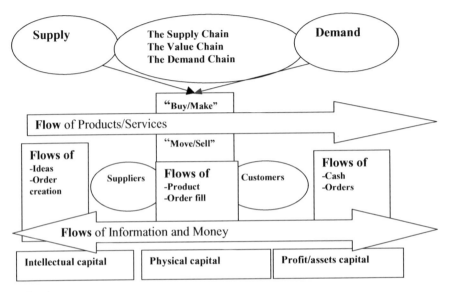

In this diagram:

- The demand chain represents the creation of demand, for example, marketing and selling with product development.
- The supply chain represents fulfilment, for example, procurement and buying, production and making with distribution and moving.
- The value chain represents performance, for example, financial measures and capital in both the internal value chain and the "extensions" upstream and downstream to the value chains of:
    - the upstream first level suppliers.
    - the first level suppliers supplier and so on, upstream.
    - the downstream customers.
    - the downstream users and final consumers.

The above activities of Buying-Making-Moving and Selling take place in business operational functions of Procurement, Production, Distribution and Marketing.

## The Supply Chain Philosophy is about networks

Each company has not only one supply chain, but many, as it deals with different suppliers and has different customers. For each individual finished product or line item, whilst some of the buying, making, moving and selling processes will be identical or very similar, the total supply chain for each product will be different, and will often involve a complex network. This goes, for example, far beyond the first supplier, and includes the supplier's supplier, then that supplier's supplier and so on.

Many organisations, in their supply management, do not work on the supply chain in this way and often stop with the first level supplier; in doing so, they overlook the fact that the supply chain is effectively a large network of many and varied supplier/customer players.

## The Supply Chain and Economic sectors

With supply chain management, therefore, there are many different supply chains to manage. These wide-reaching supply chain networks usually contain organisations from all of the main economic sectors:

- Primary sector: Raw materials from farming/fishing (food, beverages, and forestry), quarrying/mining (minerals, coals, metals) or drilling (oil, gas, water).
- Secondary sector: Conversion of raw materials into products; milling, smelting, extracting, refining into oils/chemicals/products, and possibly machining, fabricating, moulding, assembly, mixing, processing, constructing into components, sub-assemblies, building construction/ structures and furnitures/ electronic/ food/ paper/metal/ chemicals and plastic products.
- Service or tertiary sector: business, personal and entertainment services, which involve the channels of distribution from suppliers to customers, via direct, wholesale or retail channels. Services include packaging, physical distribution, hotels, catering, banking, insurance, finance, education, public sector, post, telecoms, retail, repairs etc.

Organisations will, therefore, have many supply chains both internally and externally that interact through a series of simple and complex networks.

## Procurement evolution in the Supply Chain

Procurement needs to be integrated through all of the strategic, tactical and operational levels in organisations, for example to:
- Acquire and procure what the organisation needs, by spending money externally to satisfy the needs of internal customers/users or external customers.
- Follow up on the delivery from suppliers.
- Provide information and services to internal customers (e.g. production/ manufacturing/retail shops etc.).
- Liaise, integrate and coordinate the internal supply chain.

It should be appreciated that this need for integration does not always happen in many organisations, and to take just the last point, many procurement departments just do not do this. Indeed, in many organisations, no-one does. However, this is changing as procurement evolves through the following stages:

- Stage one: Product centred procurement that was concerned with tangible products and outcomes.
- Stage two: Process centred procurement that has moved beyond stage one into process measurement.
- Stage three: Relational procurement that has expanded into purchaser/ supplier relationships.
- Stage four: Performance centred procurement that focuses on best product management and integrates relationships, processes and outcomes, which are jointly resourced with suppliers.

## Procurement and the internal offer

Procurement is therefore one part of the supply chain philosophy and in many organisations Procurement does occupy a strategic role that:

- recognises buying gives both value for money and, cost reduction.
- takes whole/holistic views over the longer term.
- uses a more integrative process approach.
- builds internal and external relationships.
- coordinates flows from suppliers into the company to meet the lead-time and availability requirements of the users/customers.

Many organisations however, actually operate their procurement activities sub-optimally and in a silo. This is because suppliers, organisations and internal business are not integrated in any meaningful way.

When this happens, the organisation really needs aligning to its core business drivers, such as customer's "needs". This, in turn, will impact the core organisational competences/capacities and will require both external and internal integration.

The following Case Study illustrates very simply some of these needed internal integration aspects.

## Case Study: Boardroom scenario

MD to Procurement Director:
"How much obsolete stock have you bought today?"
Procurement Director:
"None."

MD to Production Director:
"How much obsolete stock have you made today?"
Production Director:
"None."

MD to Sales Director:
"How many week's stock have you got?"
Sales Director:
"Three week's."
MD to Sales Director:
"How many week's stock do you need?"
Sales Director:
"One week's."

MD comments:
"Sales does not want the next two weeks' production, and production does not want what procurement is planning to buy tomorrow."

**The simple lesson:**
All internal operations should be integrated, coordinated and controlled.

In procurement, "doing the deal" alone and incrementally, is not enough, as value, risk, cost, service etc. are all involved in a complex series of trade-offs that attempt to optimise the "whole" business/supply chain. Procurement should be a part of this optimisation.

# Strategic and Corporate Procurement

## Corporate strategy

Corporate strategy links down to business strategy, which in turn links to functional strategy, for example of the procurement function. Meanwhile, the following points can be noted on the links and connections between strategies:

- Strategy is long-term, broad in scope and can be determined at corporate, business or functional levels.
- Strategy is best applied by establishing a mission or goals, assessing the organisation, assessing the environment, identifying strategic options, implementing strategy to achieve the chosen option(s).
- Continuous improvement is needed to gain competitive advantage in times of dynamic change in global markets, shortened product life cycles and more demanding customers.
- Value is essentially that perceived by the customer and is something they are prepared to pay for.

Corporate strategy is, therefore, a concept of an organisation's business, which provides a unifying theme for all its activities by asking three basic questions:

- What is the mission? What will we do and for whom will we do it (what business are we in?)

5

- What objectives do we want to achieve? (What are the goals?)
- How will we manage the activities to achieve the chosen objectives?

# Strategic management of procurement

Strategic management of procurement will need to include the following:

- Reviewing existing suppliers related to potential supply risks for the business and the spend levels.
- Identifying a number of potentially strategic suppliers.
- Examining existing activities to see if they can be outsourced.
- Developing strategic alliances, collaborations and partnerships.
- Developing strategic performance criteria.

The strategic management of procurement will need to be related to the corporate strategy and the needs of the business. For example, a business involved in trading will need to look for new products to sell; a business selling fast-moving consumer goods will look for fast, reliable suppliers. Organisations involved in continuous production will require raw material always to be available; a local public sector authority will need to demonstrate public accountability.

These differences can come from differing types of:

- Organisations; in the earlier identified primary, secondary or tertiary sectors.
- Purchases; from these three sectors.
- Organisation ownership; for example the private and the public sectors. The former is usually profit driven and therefore procurement will be required to contribute to this goal. In the public sector, a similar role to the private sector may be found in those quasi-independent/public owned organisations, such as the UK Post Office. However, the central and local government organisations, such as the NHS, are responsible to the countries population and required to obtain maximum value for a given level of cost, along with, transparency and public accountability.

A more strategic view of procurement involves recognising the following differences:

| Operational procurement | Strategic procurement |
|---|---|
| Transactional order placers | Value added facilitators |
| Short term | Long term |
| Cost focus | Customer/user focus |
| Internal view | External views |
| Performance statistics | Benchmarking |
| Technical processes | Business process |

# Procurement by the strategic requirements of the product

Once a need has been identified, the next step is to determine the importance which is applied to the product or material that is required. ABC/Pareto analysis provides a basis to identify where spends are the greatest and where the most effort should be directed to reduce costs. Here, the 80/20 rule states that, in most cases, 80% of purchase value is concentrated within 20% of the items purchased. Additionally, risk and other factors are involved.

These risk factors can be viewed from high to low, against the following criteria:

- Experience with product /service; (high risk for a new, untried products to a lower risk for repeats).
- Supply/demand balance; (short supply /excess capacity).
- Supply chain complexity; (many parties involved to "direct" purchases).
- Financial aspects of supply disruption; (high to negligible costs).
- Safety consequences of disruption; (high to low hazards).
- Design maturity; (new to established designs).
- Manufacturing complexity; (complex to simple).

The other factors can also be rated from high to low against the following criteria:

- Market structure (many sources to a monopoly supplier).
- Value of spend (high to low spending).
- Supply/demand balance (spare to no capacity).
- Efficiency of buying process (identical for all, to tailored buying).
- Development of buying process in the company (users agree specifications to cross functional reviews).
- Knowledge of suppliers pricing (cost plus to market based pricing?).

To account for both spend and risk from non-supply, due to there being few suppliers, and based on the work of Kraljic, the range of purchased items can be broken down into four categories:

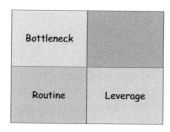

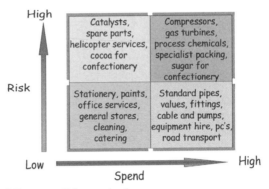

In general terms the following will be involved:

## Leverage; Low risk, high spend items
- Leverage items are those where a high volume is purchased with a high level of supplier numbers giving competition. Here, therefore, the lowest cost can easily be found. There would be a need to create competition in the marketplace for these items to drive down price. The supply market is competitive, with many available sources; hence buyers are able to leverage by maximising economies of scale and by offering large spends.

## Routine; Low risk, low spend items
- Routine buying of commodities, which required efficiency. Relationships maybe conducted at "arm's length" for these low value items. Minimal effort is needed for sourcing these items due to the relatively little impact procurement can make to reducing purchase costs. Therefore acquisition costs are targeted by the use of credit cards, EDI, internet ordering and call offs with users directed to place orders direct with the selected supplier; who reports on usage.

## Critical; High risk, high spend items
- Critical items require closer supplier relationships to ensure they are always available. These will involve usually longer term relationships and partnering approaches with suppliers. These items rank high in the Pareto analysis of spend but can also be difficult to source due to low numbers of suppliers or complex logistics. Close supplier relations are needed with possible use of joint working and multi-functional teams.

## Bottleneck; High risk, low spend items
- The need here is to ensure the supply and reduce the risk of non-supply and disruption to the business. Suppliers are often few in numbers, for example, a monopoly supplier of OEM spare parts. These items would not rate as important when analysing spend alone, but due to difficulties in sourcing there would need to be concentrated effort to secure supply of these items as the supplier often has the power.

# Levels of risks

Risk is the impact of uncertainty, and results from:

* an unexpected event, for example, a "wildcat" strike.
* false assumptions, for example, on supplier lead-time.
* human failure, for example, misinterpretations of requirements.

The sources of risk can be as follows:

* poor planning.
* not enough competent resources.
* unrealistic timescales.
* evolving technology.
* poor communication.
* insufficient task definition.
* financial restrictions.
* legislative requirements.

The level of risk will depend on a variety of factors, such as those already covered above; the strategic requirements of the product, spend and the usage, and the acceptable level of risk will therefore vary from contract to contract.

Risk can rarely be eliminated, but it can be managed or transferred to another party; the key principle is that risk should be allocated to whichever party can best manage it.

In conducting business, commercial risks will often need to be taken; and specifically for procurement, the following are examples of commercial risks:

* supplier liquidation.
* delayed delivery.
* supplier failure to meet environmental requirements.
* cost and/or price inflation.
* changes in law.

Risk factors must be identified and the probability of each risk occurring should be estimated. Risks can then be placed in rank order, with the likely impacts of each risk on success factors to be determined. The risk assessment process has the following four stages:

* identify potential problems and causal factors.
* consider possibility of problems arising.
* weight factors and assess impact.
* devise strategies to control risk.

# Procurement Strategy in the Supply Chain

As noted earlier, many organisations actually operate procurement sub-optimally. All of the value, risk, cost, service etc. are involved in a complex series of trade-offs and these must be examined with all relevant parties to optimise the "whole" business/supply chain.

Therefore, suppliers, customers and the internal business must be integrated in a meaningful way. Many organisations need aligning to their core business drivers, such as customers' needs. This, in turn, impacts on the core business competences and capacity, and will require internal integration ("win the home games first") and the removal of functional silos. Externally, this will mean developing a clear strategic view and fit of suppliers using, for example, the above Kraljic procurement portfolio analysis. The following ideal-typical table presents an overview and outline strategy for procurement. As with all ideal-typical views, it is not absolute, but is intended to demonstrate the alternative methods available and that "one size does not fit all."

| Aspect | Bottleneck items. | Critical items. | Routine items. | Leverage items. |
|---|---|---|---|---|
| Supply policy | Supplier Development<br><br>"Secure supply then Diversify" | Supplier Collaboration<br><br>"Collaborate" | Supplier Outsourcing<br><br>"Organise and let go" | Supplier Sourcing<br><br>"Play the market" |
| Overall Aim | Ensure and secure supply. After this, then search for new sources/products or services, so that can diversify from the bottleneck items. | Form closer relationships, for competitive advantage from the supply chain. | Reliable and efficient supply, using simplified ordering processes. Multi sourcing and simplified/automated / ordering process with outsourcing for these standard commodity items. | Exploit buying advantage, buy at lowest cost. Multi sourcing for these standard commodity items. |
| Supplier numbers/availability | Fewer specialist monopoly/oligopoly suppliers | Few to More suppliers | Many suppliers | Many competing suppliers |
| Power | With supplier | Interdependent | Independence | With buyer |
| Alternatives | None to few | Few to none | Many | Many |
| Costs of disruption | High | High to medium | Low | Medium to low |
| Relationships | Close with the preferred suppliers. Long term. Supply agreements. | Long term "partnerships" and collaborate with selected trustworthy and reliable suppliers. | Short term and often "distant" and "arms length." | Short term "deals" with possible long term buying consortiums, alliances, groups to concentrate buying power. |

| Aspect | Bottleneck items | Critical items | Routine items | Leverage items |
|---|---|---|---|---|
| Buyers Needs | Need security and certainty of supply. Then find alternative sources. | Need security and continuity of supply. | Need to simplify product variety and the ordering/supply process. | Need low cost supplies. |
| Product quality | Critical | Critical | Marginal | Marginal |
| Inventory/ forecasting | Repeat predictable usage. Need reliable long term forecasting. SLT is important. Likely holding of hold large stocks as insurance. | Repeat predictable usage for some items, with some random demand. Work close together to minimise stock holding. | JIT Supply. Maybe hold consignment stocks. | Possible 2 bin or VMI and JIT and consignment stocks. |
| Stock levels | Some safety stock, maybe at high levels. | Some safety stock, maybe at high levels. | Minimum | Minimum |
| Inventory method | Continuous review | Continuous review | Periodic review | Periodic review |
| Staffing | Hi level buyers with market knowledge and contingency plans. | Top level buyers in the start up, implementation and monitoring. | Low level buyers, procurement maybe actually contracted out. | Medium level buyers. |
| Sourcing methods | Elemental questionnaires. RFI/RFQ | Comprehensive questionnaires. Competitor analysis can be used. Agreements for shared risk and responsibility. | RFI/RFQ with possible ITT / competitive bidding. | Elemental questionnaires with some RFI/RFQs. ITT and competitive bidding with reverse/e auctions. |
| Terms/Enquiries | Negotiate. Availability and Supply "Rules." Term contracts. | Open book with "Partnership" / blanket agreements. | Direct Negotiations. Price and Availability "Rule". Price agreements. | Wide negotiations. "Price rules" with "wheeler dealing." Multi sourcing. |
| Orders | Standard POs. Framework agreements, medium term contracts. Quick responses. | Possible framework agreements with call offs and vendor managed inventory. | User direct call offs with agreements; otherwise spot buys / self managed with P cards /web ordering. | Standard POs. |
| Approximate UK Procurement spending | 10% | 5% | 70% | 15% |

An important aspect to consider here is how the different strategies line up and if they are consistently applied in an organisation. For example, an organisation may proclaim that quality is number one in their business, but then they select suppliers based on the lowest price. They may also say that partnership approaches are preferred, but it is actually adversary buying methods that rule.

We have also worked with an organisation where senior people were appreciative of good supplier management principles, but were then shocked to discover these were not actually being applied within the organisation – not too surprising to us when we discovered that there apparently had been no initiative of any kind undertaken to foster such principles in the organisation; this type of senior management style being called "wave a magic wand and walk".

11

We have also worked with another organisation where contract managers actually had responsibility for supplier management in their job descriptions, but most of the contract managers were not aware they actually had this responsibility, and actually believed this rested with the procurement department.

We could go on, but the point here of course, as with any strategy, is that the implementation and application is what is critical; the design is the easiest part. Merely trying to implement by "waving the wand" by the planners and strategists is damaging, wrong and can be fatal. It is a pity that more strategists in organisations (and in politics) do not recognise this simple eternal truth.

## The procurement process cycle

This cycle is that of the overall procurement process involved, and should not be viewed as being entirely what every procurement department does. For some organisations, they may be involved in everything from the start to the finish of the cycle, but for many organisations, the procurement department only has some partial involvement in the total process, for example, from taking over the need and working on the specification with the user, through to placing the order.

The procurement process follows the following stages:

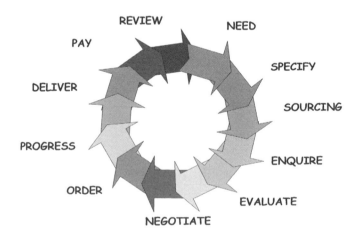

This procurement process cycle involves the following three main stages:

**The Pre-Order stage:** Need/Requirements – Specify – Sourcing – Enquiry – Evaluation – Negotiation/Selecting.

**The Order stage:** Ordering – Progressing/Expediting – Delivery/receipt.

**The Post order stage:** Payment /Invoice verification – Reviewing.

All of these stages have been already fully covered in our book *"Excellence in Procurement" (2008)* so this detail will not be covered here. However, so that we can highlight those specific aspects for Supplier Management purposes, we will briefly mention some of the relevant aspects from the Pre-order stage.

### Needs

As explained in *"Excellence in Procurement" (2008)*, an initial requisition is to be used to identify the user or customer needs, and this may range from a simple requisition covering a standard stocked product, right through to a complex project where a more thorough analysis will be carried out prior to making the final requests for products, materials and services. The need is what has to be satisfied; it represents the demand that "kickstarts" the supply chain; no demand equals no supply chain.

### Specifications

Product and service specifications will need to be identified in liaison with the user or customer. Specifications are a description of what a customer/user wants and therefore communicate what is required, to meet the needs. This is therefore a critical stage, and, as noted in *"Excellence in Procurement" (2008)*, specifications do need to be clear and communicate. The development of specifications will usually require liaison between users, procurement and maybe potential suppliers as they enable procurement to:

- Provide information on available supply.
- Provide a supplier appraisal.
- Identify risks on suppliers and products.
- Identify where the business able to standardise.

Ultimately, procurement aims to procure products and materials which are fit for purpose, and the characteristics that give this are determined by the specification. It is also important that any supplier contact is managed and controlled, and for example, it is not a good idea to have the end-users/internal customers making direct contact with suppliers with messages like, "we have a unique problem" or "we have an urgent requirement". Whilst these are a salesperson "dream" requests (consider please the salesperson's response), it also reflects an aspect of (poor) supplier management.

### Sourcing

The important aspect here for Supplier Management is that:

- The number and location of suppliers will influence the price of the goods in the marketplace.
- There are often other buyers for materials and products, and this will ensure a review by the supplier of how "attractive" the buyer could be as a customer. For example, markets may be expanding or contracting, this will influence the number of suppliers.

- The power of each party also has a part to play, for example:

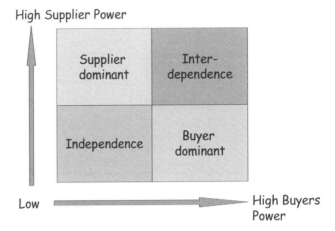

High Supplier Power

| Supplier dominant | Inter-dependence |
| Independence | Buyer dominant |

Low ⟶ High Buyers Power

This "power view" on sourcing is am important one and also relates to our earlier discussion on Kraljic. We shall be returning to this power issue again later in part 2.0 of this book.

**Enquiry & Evaluation**
As explained in *"Excellence in Procurement" (2008)*, this may take the form of pre-qualifying suppliers and is used to invite suppliers to apply for potential business. It ensures that suppliers conform to certain required criteria before further detailed information is provided to them. In making and dealing with enquiries to suppliers, approaches need to be seen as ethical, and a "level playing field" must be maintained for all proposals.

A set procedure should be laid down to deal with the response proposals based on size and spend. Analysis of the proposals can include commodity value, delivery, quality, technical merit, after-sales service, security of supply, health and safety and environmental polices. Some may determine to make enquiries by tendering; again this is more fully explained in *"Excellence in Procurement" (2008)* and involves using a formal process with the following steps:

- identification and selection of suppliers from whom to seek bids.
- issue of invitation to tender (ITT) documentation to the selected suppliers.
- receipt and assessment of tenders.
- selection of a preferred tender.

However tendering may not always give the intended open competition and fairness. Indeed tendering may be merely "going through the motions", as tendering processes can be influenced by those who have some power and influence over the eventual selection process.

Tenders may also be selectively issued and suppliers' responses are thus being influenced. In this regard, I am also reminded of a procurement manager who once said to me, "We are always able to pre-cook the tender board."

The private sector will usually disregard tendering completely and moves straight to negotiating, as they see the following disadvantages of the tendering process:

- Sometimes it is necessary to clarify technical points.
- The supplier may wish to give better alternatives that can only be found when negotiating.
- Tendering is slow and expensive to administrate and is also expensive for suppliers.
- Tendering is of no use in a "monopoly".
- Tendering conflicts with "newer" collaboration approaches and working more closely together with suppliers.
- Tendering prevents post-tender negotiations.

The supplier appraisal will be governed by the strategic significance of the product or service being sourced. The results will be based on criteria established by the purchaser in liaison with the user or customer and the purchasers' knowledge. Again *"Excellence in Procurement" (2008)* has a full discussion on the options available here, for example a detailed assessment of suppliers:

- Ability.
- Attitude.
- Organisation.
- Financial Data.
- Organisational Structure.
- Product Data.
- Supplier Production Process.

**Negotiating**

We noted earlier that the private sector will generally move straight to negotiating with suppliers and not be involved in tendering. However, as discussed in *"Excellence in Procurement" (2008)*, the public sector may also undertake direct negotiations, and we have covered there the conditions where this may occur. This book also covers, more fully, all the "mechanics" of conducting negotiations. Meanwhile, we would observe that supplier involvement would be better facilitated where negotiations move from a combative style, towards being more collaborative. This will involve moving from:

- Having one-off dealings towards longer-term dealings.
- Being opponents towards problem-solving colleagues.
- "Buy/sell" trading towards working together for mutual benefit.
- Having mistrust, bluff and suspicion in negotiations towards honesty, fairness and openness.
- Emphasising a "squeeze" on price towards working together to find solutions that reduce costs.
- Being at "opposite side of the table" towards sitting at the same side of the table.

If we were to simply view what the supplier and the customer wants, then we can see the following positions: (Source: *"The Relationship driven supply chain"*, Emmett and Crocker (2006)).

| Criteria | Suppliers want: | Customers want: |
|---|---|---|
| Orders | The "business" | Delivered/available goods/services that satisfy a requirement |
| Information | Clear requirements | Wants clear status information |
| Performance | Feedback (KPIs that are jointly measured and, benchmarked with other suppliers) | "Feed-forward" (Pre-advice and proactive status/alerts) |
| Relationship approach | "Fairness" Involvement/"Part of" | Relationships may be a reflection of the procurement portfolio and power positions |
| Price/Cost | "Fair" | The "best" total acquisition cost, total cost of ownership, life cycle cost, whole life cost (TAC/ TCO/ LCC/ WLC) |
| Quality | Clarity on what it means and what is "valued" by the customer | "Fit for purpose" |
| Delivery | On time, in full (OTIF) | On time, in full (OTIF) |
| Quantity | Large regular orders | Smaller, frequent deliveries |
| Time | Supplier lead-time | Supply lead-time |
| Place | Ex Works (International) or Factory Gate Pricing (Domestic trade) | Delivered domicile duty paid or Delivered/Carriage paid |
| Payment time | Prompt | To negotiate |

This indicates the so called "opposite" and the "them/us" scenarios. However, it also indicates that there are some very common "wants."

- Orders are the fundamental reason for the relationship, as it is the order that drives the supply chain. Customers who are very clear on their specific requirements may generate a response from their suppliers that gives alternative options. Sharing of requirements is useful; after all, suppliers "do not know what they do not know."
- Information is another common objective involving two-way communications that gives mutual understanding.
- Performance is another two-way process with feedback to suppliers on performance; and feed-forward from suppliers to customers with order status reports and pre-alerts on problems. For example the supplier advising of a delay at least enables the customer to plan; it also builds up trust, understanding and removes uncertainty. Why, for example, should customers need to expedite?
- Relationship; this is a part of this book, so there is no summary here!
- Price/cost; If total cost of ownership evaluation approaches are used, then there is really little to stop the sharing of the results with suppliers. Again, this can mean that they may be better able to suggest alternatives and options. It will also show "fairness" which, after all, is what the supplier looks for.
- Quality; Clarity and understanding will enable the meeting of requirements.
- Delivery has common measures (e.g. OTIF) for both suppliers and customers, and if both parties record these on a per transaction basis, and share such measurements openly on a period basis, they will find this enables better communications and

understanding. It also will prevent any juvenile "you did/ I did not" debates between suppliers/customers, that will eventually lead to mistrust and feelings that "they" are unreliable.

- Quantity; the differences here between the parties are "natural" and will require discussion within the overall negotiations. It may be that allowing supplier's access to demand information and forecasts, will enable the suppliers to better plan their production and so then enable the customer requirements for smaller, more frequent deliveries.

- Time; this is interesting one as, in principle, the supplier lead-time can only "kick off" after the customer's internal process in the total supply lead-time. If, therefore, the eventual users with the customer's company report continual delays in supply, it may not be always the "fault" of the actual supplier. An examination of the lead-times will indicate all of the process involved in the lead-time "chain" and emphasises the need for such an overall view.

- Place; here the assumption is that the supplier is only interested in producing/selling a product and that it is the customers responsibly to "come and get it". Meanwhile, the customers require goods delivered to them including all duties/taxes etc. Of course, it is a fact that to enable full comparisons, goods need to be costed at the place where they are to be consumed/used. Again, there is a negotiation point and an area discussed later in the book, where some buyers find an advantage in purchasing on ex-works or factory gate terms, as they then get clearer lead-time visibility and control of both the transit lead-times and freight/ logistics cost prices.

- Payment time; a clear negotiation aspect.

By exploring the above common wants, this facilitates potential mutual benefits and gains.

**Implementing Contracts**

As noted in *"Excellence in Procurement" (2008)*, it is essential, in the implementation of a contract, that all parties involved are aware of their roles and responsibilities and the contractual arrangements must be structured to match the particular requirement. Requirements can, of course, vary, and examples of different types of arrangements are found as follows:

- Spot orders are placed as and when required.
- Framework agreements for a fixed term for a specified supply, but with no initial commitment to buy, and when eventually buying, the use of call offs. There is then, an agreement to buy.
- Contracts with varied rates, dependent on certain criteria, for example, on volume quantity order, on early payment etc.

Procurement departments are usually responsible for ensuring that the best fit commercial conditions are applied to the particular purchase, and must also take account of any relevant legislative requirements. All contracts will involve the legal aspects as follows:

- Offer.
- Acceptance.

- Consideration.
- Legality.
- Capacity.

It is usually the responsibility of procurement department to ensure that:

- the appropriate terms and conditions are specified.
- there is a definition of when offer and acceptance takes place.
- there is an approved digital signature or equivalent.
- all legal principles have been followed.

With regard to the last point, *"Excellence in Procurement" (2008)* covers the main legal aspects involved, so that all parties involved are aware of their roles and responsibilities. However, beyond the mandatory legal aspects, there is a range of variations and choices to be made. What follows is an ideal-typical view to indicate this range.

Whilst for some, this idealised view will be entirely practical and realistic; for others, the following division will not be fixed and definite. There can be a mixing across this continuum and it is not therefore a "tablets of stone" view, but, is designed to show the key aspects that have to be considered before the buyer makes a choice; a choice of course that should usually be undertaken in conjunction with other internal departments in the organisation.

## Contracts types

**The buyer's views of risks include:** anything that may stop the operations of the business or prevent it from achieving its objectives, for example, poor health and safety, unreliable supplier lead-times, low product quality with high levels of defects, using new untried technology, working in political environments with constant changes to regulations, supplier closure, exchange rate variations.

**The buyer's view of rewards and benefits are:** reduces costs, improves service, quality, time to market, innovations etc.

The key aspects involved in the different contract formats are as follows:

| Aspects | Standard Contract | Framework Agreement | Open book |
|---|---|---|---|
| Other names used | Closed Fixed price | Call offs | Cost plus |
| Typical Kraljic items | Leverage and routine | Leverage, routine and bottleneck | Bottleneck and critical |
| Contract description | Standard fixed terms and conditions covering Quality, Quantity Time, Price and Delivery, plus many others, for example: -Assignment & Sub-Contracting -Arbitration -Bankruptcy -Equipment -Terms of Payment -Damages/ injury -Designs / drawings -Liability -Passing of property –Inspection / testing -Information -Copyright / Patent Rights -Statutory Regulations -Termination | There is no initial commitment to buy as the agreement just anticipates doing business. It "prepares the groundwork" and details the standard contract terms and conditions. When orders are placed by issuing a PO (known as a call off in a framework agreement), upon the order acceptance by the supplier, (without the supplier varying the terms), then there is a contract. | All costs are visible to the buyer, as the "books are open." All costs are therefore reimbursable to the supplier or maybe are paid direct by buyers. This is the "cost" aspect and the "plus" aspect can be: -a fixed management fee, or -a percentage of costs, or -agreed fees that maybe dependent on order volumes. As well as having fixed terms and conditions, there may also be some "moral" expectations/ agreements covering the preferred relational aspects. |
| Risk for buyer | Usually risks are well known and are often contractually passed to the supplier. (Although of course, any subsequent supplier failure will likely impact the buyer). | Maybe shared or maybe with the supplier. | Maybe not fully known in advance and maybe accepted by the buyer. |
| Rewards/benefits for the buyer | Perceived as being "fully protected". Penalties for supplier non conformances. Likely to be able to easily withdraw. | As for standard contract but with no initial commitment to buy. "Ready to go" immediately when wish to place orders. | Full visibility of costs and therefore all of the processes involved. Collaborative working. |
| Disadvantages for buyer | Hides supplier's profit. Supplier may include too much "contingency" cost in the price and may cut corners to improve profits. Suppliers may only do what the contract says and do not innovate or suggest improvements. | Supplier may become disappointed when, for example, they have to wait for orders which can then fall below their expectations. | Buyer needs cost knowledge. High administration. Could be little incentive for the supplier to reduce costs and improve service; however, the supplier may also do whatever is needed to make improvements, as mutual gains and goals "rule." |

| Rewards/benefits and disadvantages for the supplier | Supplier from the buyer- "you have the business, for now;" the supplier is therefore uncertain of the future. Supplier does not have to suggest any improvements. | As for standard contract but on bottleneck items, some form of incentives is available, as the buyer needs to secure supply. | Supplier incentives/ performance bonus. Incentives can follow from: -Cost reductions -Performance improvements -Delivery on time |
|---|---|---|---|
| Term | Short | Medium | Long |
| Performance expected | Standard | Satisfactory | Successful and can go beyond expectations |
| Trust | Low and is boundary trust that is determined by the contract. | Some trust beyond what the contract covers, and should become established by the reliable performances of both parties. | High and is goodwill trust. This has been built up during the working together experiences. |
| Relationships | Transactional, adversarial, contractual. | Cooperative | Collaborative, strategic alliance, mutuality, commitment. |
| Contract price | Known /fixed by price agreements | Fixed by the PO/contract, but may not have been initially fixed in the agreement. | Cost plus. The total cost price may be estimated in advance and therefore may become a variable if the estimating was wrong. |
| Buyer controls after orders have been placed | Low efforts needed as measures by non compliance and can easily change suppliers if needed. | Low to medium effort needed | High effort needed and both parties may measure and jointly agree remedial actions |
| Control of costs | With supplier | With supplier | With buyer |

It should be noted here that Open Book has been criticised as not being transparent enough, and is only one-way, and that it should be more open by being on a more transparent two-way method. Suffice to say, the above Open Book description does actually cover cost transparency and collaboration and is, therefore, two-way working; we will however return to this debate later.

Meanwhile a good contractual legal agreement may therefore provide:

- the overall groundwork and framework for the future supply.
- a perceived feeling that we have minimised risk and have a "safety umbrella".
- a formal "place of last resort" to resolve any ensuing problems.

However, legal agreements will not prevent problems, nor will they provide protection on a daily working basis. Legal agreements will only provide a formal structured framework for handling problems that have already occurred. Any problem handling may, of course, be handled without recourse to any formal legal involvement/judgements, as legal costs can be high/prohibitive and involve long time scales/delays.

Small wonder that some may question why the initial time and cost, in agreeing legal agreements, is entered into in the first place? It is also not unusual to find one party will quickly agree to the tabled terms to prevent these expenses. Additionally, they may also agree because one party has the power to force through their terms. However, as explained in *"Excellence in Procurement" (2008)*, the use of industry standard terms and conditions will mitigate these set-up expenses.

Indeed, we suggest later that, for complex purchases, most of the value obtained from the supplier is actually going to be driven by the post-contract management, rather than from the upfront negotiated contractual terms.

It can also be seen that the different types of contracts have connections to Kraljic and therefore to procurement strategy and the relationships aspects. Suffice to note that a successful relationship is mainly made not only on legal contracts, but on aspects like trust, fairness, respect, promises and mutual benefits that occur daily between all of the players involved. It is how these are handled that will determine successful supplier management; success is often unlikely to be because of the rigour of the legal contract.

**Who is responsible for the pre-order stage?**
This stage covers Need/Requirements – Specify – Sourcing – Enquiry – Evaluation – Negotiation/Selecting that all work towards the implementation of a contract and order placing.

The level of a procurement department's involvement in managing contracts must be established, for example, who has responsibility for:

- Support and advice; for example the decision on which source to use may be with the budget holder/end user or, if the product has not been sourced before, then there may be an opportunity to develop a supplier.
- Contract negotiation; here it could be the direct responsibility of the buyer to negotiate terms and conditions on behalf of the user or internal customer.
- Contract management; who should have the responsibility to manage the total procurement process from identifying the need, agreeing specifications, identifying potential suppliers, supplier appraisal, contract negotiations and contract implementation, including the performance measurement.
- Collaborative partnerships will also need to be based on trust and cooperation, shared information and shared goals, and without these, then the partnership merely becomes a long-term contract.

It is important that organisations determine who owns the relationship with suppliers. The standard answer, if there is such a thing, but one that is often given by people during our training courses/consultancy assignments, is that as the need is determined by the user, then the user, or their delegated person, has such responsibility. In textbook terms, and theoretically, this seems entirely logical.

However, in organisations where the responsibility is ill-defined, or where schoolyard politics have a part to play, it can happen that most users will choose to believe that it is actually the procurement department that has the responsibility for the relationship with suppliers. They also often believe this to be true without making any formal delegation; therefore they have a viewpoint of "after all, we passed it on to you, so get on with it."

Whilst one can fully appreciate that the procurement department is involved in sourcing and finalising the deal, it should not be the case that procurement are systematically left to do this in a vacuum and in total isolation from the rest of the organisation. Unfortunately, however, the authors know of too many examples where this actually happens.

Let us, in the meanwhile, further examine the objectives of the procurement process, and make the important point that these objectives do not necessarily equate to only one functional department in an organisation.

## Procurement objectives and the five rights

A classic definition of procurement is the five rights:

*"Securing supplies, materials, and services of the right quality in the right quantity at the right time from the right place (source) at the right cost."*

It should be appreciated that the Five Rights, (quality, quantity, time, place and price) are inter-related and are not mutually exclusive. Using them however, ensures that all aspects have been considered, and the priority by which the rights are applied can also be dictated by organisational strategy and the requirements of the business. It is these requirements that are the driver for procuring.

It is important to note here that these requirements are not those of the procurement department, but are those of the business; the procurement department being an internal service provider that works towards meeting such ends.

Meanwhile another aim for procurement is:

*"To obtain bought in goods/services at the lowest acquisition cost."*

The total acquisition cost (TAC) concept emphasises that more than the cost price is involved, and we shall be examining this important concept soon, but let's first look at each of the five rights. Again, it should be appreciated that these five rights apply for the business, additionally, as we will explain, the five rights also become critical in determining key performance indicators for the procurement process and in turn, the success of the overall supplier management process.

### The Right Quality
Quality is the degree of level of excellence as perceived by the customer; meanwhile it may also be viewed as the product or service being "fit for purpose" and also "performing right first time every time". These involve:

- Meeting requirements.
- Fitness for purpose.
- Minimum variance.
- Elimination of waste.
- Continuous improvement culture.

The right quality should be agreed by the buyer with their customer. Whilst their customer will be restricted by design, performance or safety factors, the buyer will be restricted by costs and market competition. From the buyer's perspective, the quality agreed should allow for competition between suppliers.

**The Right Quantity**

The right quantity to be ordered by the buyer and being sold by the supplier will attempt to balance the requirements of both parties. If taking a wider procurement/supply chain management view, then possibly collaboration or partnership methods may well be used in the supplier/customer relationship to better balance the requirements.

Lower prices can be negotiated for larger quantities, but this may conflict with storage capabilities and production requirements. Dependent or independent demand can also be established prior to assessing the quantities needed; these being simply, demand that is dependent on something else (for example car tyres supplied to car assemblers is dependent on the assemblers production plan), or car tyres supplied to the replacement/repair market. The former dependent demand is more definite and certain, and the latter independent demand is more random and uncertain.

**The Right Time (to buy and to deliver)**

The right time to buy will be influenced by the following factors:

- Availability.
- Market conditions.
- Competition.
- Procurement policies.
- Customer Demand.

The right time to deliver will be influenced by:

- Supply lead-time (from "initial need" to "available for use").
- Organisational requirements.
- Customer demand.

In a production environment, the right time to deliver will need to coincide with production schedules, where any failure/lead-time variability could have serious consequences to the production schedules and also to the raw material inventory levels. In a retail environment, the right time to deliver will ideally be organised to coincide with low to zero stock holding in the retail store so that non-availability "on-shelf" does not occur.

### The Right Place

Buyers need to ensure that the products or services are bought from the right supplier upstream in the supply chain. Once the source has been identified, the market conditions will need to be assessed and a formal supplier appraisal may be needed, depending on spend, volume and risk.

Downstream, it is also often the responsibility of buyer to ensure that the materials, products or services are delivered to the right place. So, for example, buyers will need to ensure that the correct delivery details are provided by the user/customer, and that the supplier has the comprehensive delivery details.

### The Right Price

Information on prices should be gathered to allow full analysis of market prices. For example, raw material prices could be monitored, not only for the purchase of the actual raw materials, but also for when raw material prices may affect the cost of products that are being bought.

Key factors in the total price need to be understood and broken down and these would include direct and indirect costs along with the profit margin. Where capital equipment is being purchased, a Total Cost of Ownership approach (TCO) should be applied.

# Total Cost of Ownership

This is a costing philosophy that also includes value, as the Total Cost of Ownership viewpoint sees the benefit of ownership will only come when the value added to the business through owning the asset is greater than the TCO. The value added, therefore, is where the benefits are greater than the TCO; conceptually described as:

TCO = Price + total acquisition cost (TAC) + life cycle costs (LCC) or whole life costs (WLC).

Both TAC and WLC are examined below.

**Total acquisition cost (TAC)** is the Price Paid plus all other costs, for example:

| | | |
|---|---|---|
| • | Quality | e.g. errors, defects, returns |
| • | Delivery | e.g. modes, time scales |
| • | Delivery Performance | e.g. non availability, unreliability |
| • | Lead-time | e.g. stock financing |
| • | Packing | e.g. point of display repack |
| • | Warehousing | e.g. extra handling |
| • | Inventory | e.g. product deterioration |
| • | New Supplier | e.g. start-ups, assessments |
| • | Administration | e.g. order processing |

The question to be answered is: Exactly what are all these costs, beyond the price paid?

**Whole life costing (WLC)** is the same as Life Cycle costing and can be defined as:

*"The systematic consideration of all relevant costs and revenues associated with the acquisition and ownership of the asset."*

Essentially, WLC is a means of comparing options and their associated cost and revenue over a period of time. The elements to be costed include:

- Initial capital/procurement costs; e.g. design, construction, installation, purchase, or leasing fees and charges.
- Future costs; e.g. all operating costs (rent, rates, cleaning, inspection, maintenance, repair, placements/renewals, energy, dismantling, disposal, security, and management). It should be noted that unplanned and unexpected maintenance/ refurbishment may amount to more than half of the initial capital spent.
- Opportunity costs; e.g. the cost of not having the money available for alternative investments, which would earn money, or the interest payable on loans to finance work.

The importance of TCO, TAC and WLC is that they go beyond looking only at the cost price, and emphasise that there is more involved than, say, the lowest cost. As has been said, if everyone purchased on a lowest price basis, then every car on the road would be a (whatever the lowest priced car in your country is).

Factors affecting the immediate cost of acquisition are as follows:

- initial price.
- cost of financing.
- terms of payment.
- performance and technical guarantees.
- liquidated damages.
- conformance with programme.

Medium-term WLC considerations are as follows:

- build costs.
- running costs.
- costs of spares.
- operation and maintenance costs.
- after-sales service/support.

Long-term WLC considerations meanwhile are:

- component replacement life.
- retro-fitting costs.
- dismantling costs.
- disposal costs.

# The 5 Rights and Supplier/Buyers

The five rights connect customer/internal users, buyers and suppliers. The following commonalities can be identified:

## Quality

Clarity with suppliers will better enable the meeting of quality requirements. Customers who are very clear on their specific requirements may generate a response from their suppliers that gives them some alternative options.

Sharing of requirements is therefore useful; after all, suppliers "do not know what they do not know". Suppliers can then deliver the appropriate quality required, and in accordance with a negotiated "right price." Quality needs to be designed into products or services before they are supplied; as has been said, you cannot inspect quality into a product. The time spent on receipt by buyers/users/customers, for the majority of purchases, in the detailed checking of product quality, such as the opening and counting and quality checking of individual items, is often therefore just totally wasted and non-value added time. Whilst external checks for transit damage can be made, product quality is designed into products by suppliers and most certainly, those organisations working collaboratively with suppliers or receiving goods on a just in time basis, ensure that this is the case.

## Quantity

It is the placing of an order quantity that triggers the buyer/supplier relationship. Order size differences between the parties will require discussion. It may be that allowing suppliers access to demand information and forecasts will enable them to better plan their production and stock levels and enable them to better match the buyers' requirements for smaller more frequent deliveries.

## Time

In the total supply lead-time, the supplier's lead-time only starts after the all of customer's internal processes have been completed. If therefore, buyers/customers are reporting supply lead-time delays or variations in the supply lead-times, then it may not be always the "fault" of the actual supplier. An examination of lead-times will, therefore, indicate all the process involved in the lead-time "chain." Supply lead-time is a critical aspect of procurement and has been examined in *"Excellence in Procurement" (2008)* and, additionally, the practical applications into ordering/inventory levels are also comprehensively covered in *"Excellence in Inventory Management" (2007)*.

## Place and delivery

There are two extreme options/assumptions here:
1.   The supplier is only interested in producing/selling a product and therefore it will be the customers responsibly to "come and get it" on an EXW (ex-works) Incoterms basis.
2.   The customers do not want to be involved until they receive the product and therefore require the supplier to deliver the goods to them, including payment of all the duties/taxes etc.; using DDP (Delivered Duty Paid) Incoterms basis.

To enable full comparisons between these two extremes, goods will need to be costed at the place where they are to be consumed/used. This can be a negotiation point, as some customers do find an advantage in buying from suppliers on ex-works terms. Here then, they get clearer lead-time visibility and control of both the transit lead-times and freight/ logistics cost prices.

This important decision in procurement/importing, is examined more fully in part two of the book, under "Handling orders and Progressing and Delivery".

It should also be appreciated that delivery has common key performance indicators for both the supplier (on the outbound delivery) and the customer (on the inbound delivery) such as on-time, in-full. If both parties are able to record these on a per transaction basis, and then share such measurements openly and periodically, they will find that this enables better communications and understanding.

### Cost/price
If total cost of ownership evaluation approaches are used, then there is really little to stop the sharing of the results with suppliers. Again, this can mean that they may be able to better suggest alternatives and options. It will also show "fairness," which is what many suppliers look for.

## The 5 Rights and Key performance indicators

These KPIs must be determined, and are discussed more fully in Part 3.0 of this book. Suffice to note here that the determining and handing over of KPIs to monitor the following delivery activity, follows from the order stage. The order stage "sets the scene" for how the subsequent contract and orders should be handled. Accordingly, time spent now in determining and agreeing KPIs with all the relevant players is time well spent to prevent subsequent confusion and disputes. This may well involve determining service level agreements.

### Service Level Agreements (SLAs)
These can be defined as the following:

*"A contract that defines the relationship between a supplier and a customer."*

*"A negotiated agreement designed to create a common understanding about service."*

SLAs set objective targets that prioritise needs and wants by defining what is acceptable, for both supplier and customer. SLAs attempt to clarify the following:

- What is expected?
- What the supplier will supply/deliver?
- How often will it be supplied?
- To what quality standards will it be supplied?
- At what price?
- What are the supplier's obligations?
- What is the recourse for both parties if things go wrong?

Typical clauses in SLAs are as follows:
- Service description.
- Service levels.
- Duration.
- Reporting levels.
- Level monitoring.
- Performance standards.
- Review meetings/frequency.
- Dispute resolution.
- Termination.

# Supplier Management in the Procurement process

We introduced the following diagram earlier, to illustrate simply that the main parties in the procurement process need connecting, and that supplier management is needed to make this connection.

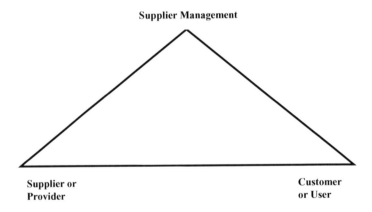

A valid proxy for supplier management is contract management, and a report by the Aberdeen Group *(The Contract Management Benchmark Report - Procurement Contracts, March 2006.)* indicates just what organisations need to consider when making the above connection. A summary of the report follows:

- Define and communicate procedures for the administration of contracts.
- Ensure executive and stakeholder support.
- Increase collaboration amongst internal stakeholders.
- Define information and reporting requirements comprehensively.
- Invest in management process capabilities.

This report also indicates what happens when there is poor contract management. A summary follows with our views on what is needed:

| Issue | Impacts | Needs |
|---|---|---|
| Fragmented procedures | Users maverick buying<br>Increased finance and supply risk<br>Under leveraged spending | Internal liaison<br>Kraljic segmentation |
| Labour intensive and bureaucratic processes | Long supply lead-times | Internal and external liaison |
| Poor visibility into contracts and terms | Poor compliance<br>Inconsistent terms<br>Poor spend analysis | Influence suppliers<br>Internal liaison |
| Ineffective compliance monitoring | High price variance<br>Overpayments<br>Performance risks | Agreed KPIs<br><br>Work with suppliers |
| Inadequate performance analysis | Policy and regulation violations | Agreed KPIs |

To give direction to a supplier management initiative, having clarity of vision, principles and values is helpful. These are all related and connected, where for example; a vision is a view of the required future state, and gives direction towards this future. A vision describes:

- Where you want to be.
- What you want to create.
- What you can commit to.
- What you believe in.

What we believe in is represented by our beliefs; these are those ultimate truths that are the "bottom line" below which we will not go. Besides beliefs, visions also contain values or principles, which provide the directional journey and guidance towards achieving the vision. Beliefs are at the very foundation of a vision, and where beliefs and vision are in variance, the vision will be difficult to achieve as it will not be supported by the belief systems of those involved in furthering and achieving it.

Having clarity of beliefs and values is vitally important; points well noted by John Harvey Jones:

> "I believe that the organisations which get most out of their people are those whose values are consistent, or, at minimum, harmonious with each other. The starting point to achieve this managerial nirvana lies in ensuring that the value systems of the business are congruent with the values and aspirations of the individuals."

> "Unless the values are lived up to at every level, unless the systems support the values, unless those who are promoted are seen to espouse and buy into the concepts, value statements are a massive switch off."

> **(Source: Sir John Harvey Jones)**

When handling relationships, having a clear statement of principles will bring clarity to how the business relationships should be handled. Simply, but critically, it shows what we believe in.

The following is one example of a *"Statement of Principles"* used in dealing with suppliers:

- *Our relationship will be ethical and progressive.*
- *Our relationship will adopt continuous learning and improvement (what's wrong, and how to fix it) as a fundamental philosophy.*
- *We will commit to communicate, as communication is about all having mutual understanding and is therefore a two-way process.*
- *We will commit to behaviour which:*
  - *openly shares ideas, listens and exchanges information;*
  - *is mutually trusting, mutually understanding, honest and respectful of differences;*
  - *shows an unconditional positive regard for people*
- *We do have a common cause, we have much to learn from each other, we will talk and listen, we will not blame, we are survivors in the same boat.*

Values and principles can also come from the collective aspirations and the shared commitment of the people involved in the process. An example follows:

*We, as a Team, committed to the following at place x on y date:*

- *We will use the "right" language in all our external dealings with others.*
- *We will be "open" with each other in the team.*
- *We will support each other, especially in front of others.*
- *We will have the confidence to confront each other.*
- *We will deliver quality work.*

This statement was actually generated during a team building training session and was signed by all of the team members. It, therefore, provided an on-going record of the commitments made and was visibly framed and used as a public reference point. It effectively provided a statement of the teams' personality.

## Objectives of Supplier Management

Considering the above, we can see that the objectives of supplier management include the following:

- Management of the relationship to achieve agreed KPIs between the supplier/provider and the customer/user.
- Liaise with all internal departments to facilitate the above, for example, the finance, procurement, logistics departments.
- Liaise with all the suppliers internal departments to facilitate the above, for example, finance, procurement, logistics.
- Influence the supplier to achieve benefits for the customer/user.
- Listen to the supplier and assist them to achieve benefits.
- Work together for continuous improvement to achieve additional benefits.
- Anticipate changes to internal business needs or from external developments.

- Be alert to the need to plan a replacement supplier, or, the renewal of the existing contract.

The following top 5 reasons (**Source:** *Aberdeen Group "Sell Side Contract Management"*, *December 2007*) have also been noted as reasons for having supplier relationship management:

1.  Reduce revenue leakage due to non compliances.
2.  Assess and mitigate risks.
3.  Continuity management over a long time scale.
4.  Improve customer relationships.
5.  Better meeting of commitments and obligations.

These objectives all involve suppliers and have led us to think that there is a need for organisations to consider providing supplier service.

## The Future: Supplier Service

Organisations are now well versed in customer service, indeed the customer *is* the business for many. This was not always true, but now the growth and acceptance of the importance of customer service is generally well recognised (if not always well practiced!).

At the other extreme from customers, we have suppliers, and as supplier service is a concept very similar to customer service, then it may be usefully considered. It presents some interesting and possibly controversial views, as this book is very much about trying to ensure that supplier management becomes as well recognised as customer service. Hopefully, it will also be well practiced; meanwhile, let us amplify supplier service/management further.

The supply chain is also the supply-demand chain and also the supplier-customer chain. The supply chain can also be visualised as a series of connected links of suppliers and customers:

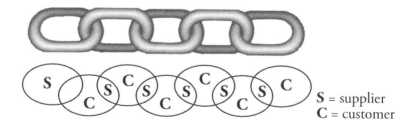

S = supplier
C = customer

There are many and multiple supplier/customer connections in any supply chain. Such connections can be internal or external, involving internal departments in an organisation, or external suppliers or customers.

For example, the passing on of paperwork to the next person, the passing on of a sub-assembly on an assembly line or the supply of component part from an external supplier.

Of course, and to state the obvious, suppliers have customers and customers have suppliers and additionally, one may be a customer in one transaction, and then a supplier in another transaction.

Suppliers will, naturally and normally, view the next connection link as a customer. However, rarely will customers view their suppliers in the same way as they do their customers. Yet in the supply chain process, they are both connected dependently. If buyers would see suppliers the same as they see customers, then supply chain relationships should change and, resulting, overall, in an end service to the ultimate end customer which should be "perfect."

This is what we have called supplier service. Whilst we do not really want to add to the multitude of jargon that already exists in our profession, it is our belief that seeing suppliers in a similar way to how we already see customers will bring a paradigm shift in our thinking.

Seeing suppliers this way, therefore, will mean that the following rules and actions have to apply with suppliers:

**Supplier Service Rules**

- Believe that suppliers possess good ideas.
- Gather supplier feedback at every opportunity.
- Focus on continual improvement.
- Actively solicit good and bad feedback.
- Don't spend vast sums of money doing it.
- Seek real-time feedback.
- Make it easy for suppliers to provide feedback.
- Leverage technology to aid your efforts.
- Share supplier's feedback throughout the organisation.
- Use feedback to make changes quickly.

**Definitions of Supplier Service**
Supplier service can be variably seen and the following five views represent some different definitions:

**1. Supplier service is seen as a need satisfier**
*"Supplier Service is a function of how well an organisation meets the needs of its suppliers."*

**2. Supplier service is seen as taking care**
*"Supplier Service is a phrase that is used to describe the process of taking care of our suppliers in a positive manner."*

**3. Supplier service is seen as keeping promises**
*"Supplier service is the ability to provide them with feedback in the way that it has been promised."*

### 4. Supplier service is seen as adding value
*"Supplier service is a process for providing competitive advantage and adding benefits in order to maximize the total value."*

*"Supplier service is the commitment to providing value added services to external and internal suppliers, including attitude knowledge, technical support and quality of service in a timely manner."*

### 5. Supplier service is seen as all of the supplier contact
*"Supplier service is any contact between a supplier and a company, which causes a negative or positive perception by a supplier."*

## Total supplier service

Top leadership must have the commitment to suppliers, and supplier focussed procedures will need to be in place. What is important to accept is that the supplier is:

*   a part of the business.
*   an important person to have contact with.
*   one we depend on.
*   a human being with feelings and emotions.
*   not one to win arguments with, but someone who can help us to build our business and give us a competitive advantage.

## Supplier Satisfiers

All suppliers will expect, as a minimum, the following:

*   Reliability.
*   Responsiveness.
*   Accessibility.
*   Accuracy.

Providing suppliers with the above will prevent them from being dissatisfied. However these will not, by themselves, provide satisfaction. To provide supplier satisfaction, the following is required:

*   Fully meet their expectations (and therefore prevent dissatisfaction).
*   Responsiveness.
*   Courtesy.
*   Empathy.
*   Provide exceptional quality.
*   Good people relationships.
*   Delivery of value.
*   Handle any complaints well.
*   Obtain the repeat business.

**Supplier Perception**

One of the obvious difficulties in meeting supplier's expectations is that "Perception is Reality." Therefore, we are entering into human variability and subjectivity. Everything that is done for suppliers will be the suppliers perception, and how they perceive it is real to them. A buyer's reality should, therefore, be the supplier's perception of the buyer's performance.

Many people are, however, uncomfortable with this "reality check", and see it as an unsolvable problem in relation to whatever "normal" buying is supposed to be.

One very clear reality (and often one not recognised) is that attitudes and feelings will definitely affect the way any service delivery is perceived. Accepting this view will require some flexibility from management, such as giving discretion to staff to deal with suppliers, and not only relying on any standard and fixed structural procedural manuals and guidelines. After all, suppliers are individuals and organisational procedures must support this. Service is all about delivering: not only what it is like doing business with your organisation, but also with you personally. Feelings and attitudes are an important aspect.

**The importance of attitudes**

Please consider the following diagram:

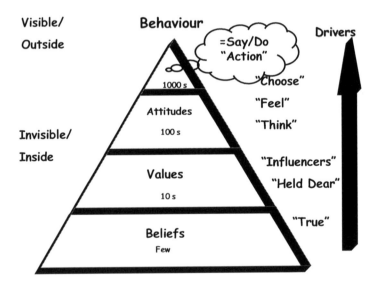

Our attitudes are underpinned by our beliefs and values, and will work through into how we behave (defined here as what we say or do).

We will therefore tend to judge from our perspective alone, and will not always consider the other parties fully enough.

Good supplier-focussed people will have a deep belief that supplier service is important, they will value this and will then lead by example, so that this belief will then work through into their attitudes and be shown and reflected by what they say and what they do. Good supplier-focussed people will therefore:

- pull more than push.
- be two-way communicators.
- makes concessions: "I think this, but what do you think?".
- problem solve and explore interests.
- hold views and reasons that "working together works" and is the best approach.

Of course, the opposite is also true; often when buyers report problems with suppliers, this can be because they do not have a belief that suppliers are important. As has been said by Henry Ford: "If you think you can or think you cannot, you are right."

Simple perhaps, but profound in its application, and to changing what is done with suppliers. When beliefs are impacted and changed then other changes will automatically result.

**Supplier complaints**
Common complaints from suppliers are when the following happens:

- Their expectations are not met; e.g. a delayed payment.
- Inflexible responses has been received; e.g. when a procurement department (the only department the supplier has had contact with), makes a response to a delayed payment enquiry by saying, it is "nothing to do with me, it is the accounts department".
- Mistakes have been made; e.g. forgetting to say something has changed.
- Communications are poor; e.g. telling one way with no listening and checking understanding.
- Delays have been made in payment; e.g. cash flow is critical in all business, cash flow problems are a major source of company failure/bankruptcy, therefore unplanned delays mean supplier cash flow problems. Where however these delays are known in advance, then suppliers may "compensate" by charging higher prices, reducing service levels, look for alternative customers or even withdraw from the business.
- Dealing with unprofessional people; e.g. "we have just given the supplier a bloody nose" (an overheard buyer's comment).

**The Supplier Service-focussed organisation**
To move towards being be a supplier service-focussed organisation, it is necessary to know:

- Who your suppliers are.
- What they expect and need from you.
- How well you are meeting their expectations.
- How to provide supplier care and follow up.
- What needs to be done to make improvements.
- What are the barriers to making these improvements.
- How you can remove these barriers.

The following view of a supplier service-focussed and non-supplier-focussed organisations shows the differences and what is important:

| Supplier service focus | Non supplier focus |
|---|---|
| Profit comes from supplier and customer satisfaction | Profit comes first, then supplier and customer satisfaction |
| Preventing problems | Detecting problems |
| Explicit standards | Vague standards |
| Complaints are seen as a chance to learn | Complaints are a nuisance |
| Run by people working with other people using systems, if appropriate | Runs by systems and procedures and then people |

The supplier service-focussed organisation will have the following five key attributes:

• Reliability: Dependable, accurate performance consistently and in all of the details
• Ownership: Front line ownership, so that those who receive complaints are also able to sort them out.
• Responsiveness: Clear evidence of a willingness to help.
• Attitudes: Courtesy, friendly, empathy and caring by employees for the suppliers "unique" requirements.
• Appearance: Clean and tidy facilities, equipments, people etc.

**Benefits of good supplier service**
As can been seen, the road to improving supplier service may not be easy; however the benefits can be huge and longlasting. The following benefits will all make contributions to the survival, well-being and the profitability of any organisation:

• Reliable service with a marketable product with a price difference.
• Market changes, can be better handled and managed.
• Continuous improvement becomes a part of the culture, with innovative and responsive staff.
• A positive view of your organisation from shareholders, the community and potential employees, with competitors who "fear" your organisation.
• Suppliers who now see the organisation as:
  - responsive and listening
  - collaborative and sharing
  - understanding what is critical to their own success
  - "good people to deal with"

The way suppliers are handled is therefore fundamental to Supplier Management and the following will give another view on this.

**Supplier Approaches**
The following questions can be asked to give an indication on the approaches that are being used with suppliers:

**Supplier approach questionnaire**
Score: 1 to 10 as follows:  1 = totally agree with list A
                            5 = neither
                            10 = totally agree with list B

|  | List A | List B | Score |
|---|---|---|---|
| Suppliers are called | Vendors | Partners | |
| Approach with suppliers | "Attack/Defend" | Collaborative and problem solving. | |
| Dependency | Independent | Inter-dependence | |
| Risk | All is externalised to suppliers | Shared and open | |
| Outcome | Self survival | Mutual survival | |
| Controls | KPIs are used for control and compliance actions. | Mutual agreed KPIs, discussions on shortfalls and remedial actions. | |
| Contracts | Legal contracts | Moral agreements | |

**Score: From 7 to 70 = _____**

**Explanation**
7 to 34: List A favoured: Combative approach
35 totally neutral
36-70:  List B favoured: Collaborative approach

**To change the approach/ways forward:**
1.  understand the current position
2.  understand the gap between where we want to be
3.  understand what drives the differences in the two positions
4.  understand to change from the current "Status Quo" will require change to beliefs and values and attitudes
5.  create an action plan

# The three supply chain roles

Following from the above discussion on supplier service, this leads us to conclude that all organisations have three roles in supply chains; these are as a:

1.  Supplier.
2.  Customer.
3.  Value creator.

With the first two roles, we need to see the connections and the effects that both of these roles have. For example, as we have just explored above, what would change if we were to see suppliers in the same way that we view customers?

As has been shown above, some of the most important principles of offering such supplier service are therefore exactly the same as customer service principles, these being:

- Suppliers (and customers) have needs and expectations.
- Supplier (and customer) service can be a source of competitive advantage.
- Supplier (and customer) service is always delivered by people, so how they do it, is more important, than what the product/service being delivered actually is.
- Supplier (and customers) offer different levels of service.

The third role in supply chains of being a value creator is where each party in the supply chain is able to create value. This has two aspects:

- Value is found when something; satisfies a need, conformed to expectations and/ or, gives "pride of ownership", i.e. it is "valued" over something that is not. Here then the perception of value will differ. Maybe value is, simply, what the customer says it is; as customers will have different perceptions of "worth" and "price." For example, different customers have different perceptions of quality/lead-time and the cost/service balance. Maybe therefore, value can be seen at the balance/pivot points between worth and price, quality and lead-time and cost and service?
- Value is also the opposite to cost and in most processes, more time is actually spent on adding cost and not on adding value. A business will not find it worthwhile to invest and automate wasteful non-value added activities. Waste is the symptom rather than the root cause of the problem. Attention should therefore be given to those activities that do add "real" value, for example:
  - Make it faster, through form changes (e.g. redesign a product)
  - Move it faster, through time changes (e.g. shorten the transit time)
  - Get paid faster, through place changes (e.g. sell Ex-Works)
  - Serving the customer better

A supply chain view of added value would also recognise that it is only the movement to the customer that is adding (the ultimate) value. Stopping or delaying the flow adds costs. As it is only the movement to the customer that adds the ultimate value, smooth continuous flow movements must be preferable.

**Value and competitive advantage**
As is now well recognised, supply chains compete as well as individual organisations, and, increasingly, it is the supply chain that brings competitive advantage for many organisations. In turn, competitive advantage can be seen as being a cost leader or a service/value leader; as shown by the following comparison where the former is essentially represented by a lean supply chain and the latter by an agile supply chain (these types of supply chain will be covered soon).

| Cost Leadership – give same standard products/service at a lower price "Do it cheaper" and Waste Minimised | Product or Service Leader – give products or services that cannot be found anywhere else "Do it better" and Value Added |
|---|---|
| Standard products Standard offering | Customer designed product/services Value added bespoke offering |
| Production push Flow and mass volume production, with high mechanisation | Market pull Job shop production with low mechanisation |
| Low inventory levels | Flexible inventory |
| Focus on productivity and efficiency | Focus on creativity and innovation |
| Stable planning | Flexible planning |
| Lowest possible costs with service a constraint | Maximises innovation responses/service with cost a constraint |
| Lead-time reduction | Short lead-times/quick responses |
| Minimise waste | Maximise service |

These two positions can be expanded as follows, where it can be seen that it is possible, if not easy in practice, to offer both cost and service/value leadership.

# Competitive advantage

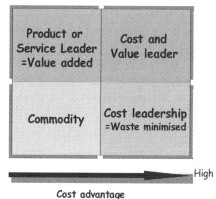

Differentiation

Product or Service Leader =Value added | Cost and Value leader

Commodity | Cost leadership =Waste minimised

High

Cost advantage

**Value creation involves suppliers**

The challenges to be faced in value creation will basically involve doing things faster, for example, making products quicker, moving them into the marketplace faster and getting paid faster. Supplier rationalisation on the basis of product quality and reliability in lead-time and delivery performance is, therefore, required. This means facing up to challenges such as:

- Reducing inventory.
- Responsive order processing.
- Short and reliable last times; it is not just the supplier lead-time but the overall supply lead-time from all those involved in all processes.
- Product received that is the "right quantity, right quality, at the right time and the right cost."
- Using appropriate ICT.
- Close working relationships and understanding of all the supply chain "players".

This focuses, for a specific supply chain, on all of the current material and information lead-times, the storage/static times and the payment/credit times; as well as the associated customer service requirements of availability, delivery schedules/ frequencies and the requirement to provide customers/users with continuous reliability over a long time period.

How well all of these aspects are managed will actually affect profit and a business strategy. Suppliers are also connected into this, as shown in the following diagram:

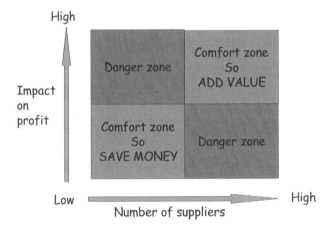

Clearly suppliers should be consciously and better joined up to their clients' business; we believe this must be more actively considered by many organisations, so that the links between suppliers and customer service will then be better managed.

### Value, relationships and exchanges

Adding value and value creation is rarely going to be achieved by single views or by one party. As we have shown above, value creation is a two-way street that involves parties making choices in how they can work together by deciding what relationship is required, and what needs to be exchanged between each party.

Exchanges here are anything that is exchanged between suppliers and buyers/users/customers so that value is created for mutual benefit, for example:

- People, e.g. on secondments, job swaps etc.
- Materials, e.g. designs, joint procurement.

- Plant and equipment, e.g. sharing.
- Money, e.g. loans, investments.
- Information, e.g. patents, real time access to each others systems.
- Methods of work, e.g. ideas, different ways.

Looking at the short and long term positions of value creation related to relationships and exchanges, such connections can be seen as follows:

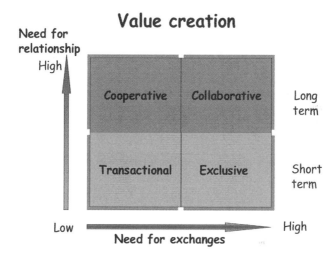

The varied positions above are amplified below:

| Position | Need for relationship | Need for exchanges | Comments | Examples |
|---|---|---|---|---|
| Transactional | Low | Low | Each party having separate main goals and are only together for a short term deal | Routine and leverage items. |
| Exclusive | Low | High | Needs some specific exclusive exchange for only a short time | New product launch. |
| Cooperative | High | Low | Working together is needed to secure supply, but there is little need for exchanges | Bottleneck items. |
| Collaborative | High | High | Both parties are in it for mutual gain and have open access to each others resources | Critical items. |

As already noted, adding value and value creation is rarely going to be achieved by just the one party, and requires suppliers to be connected with customers/users/buyers. Where there is any dissatisfaction, then this needs working at, unless of course, power plays are in force that prevent this happening. If such power plays do happen, then possibly full value creation is going to be prevented.

Accordingly, making such connections will take the view that suppliers are like "cogs in the machine" and cannot be viewed as being "easily replaceable." Additionally, replacement

41

suppliers may not be available now or "forever", and losing a supplier may cost sales and customers. Harnessing the supplier's knowledge can therefore add value to both organisations.

## Varied supplier/customer requirements

If we look at the 5 rights related to Kraljic, we can see that buyers actually have a hierarchy of requirements. This is shown below:

| The Right | Bottleneck/critical items Aim: Secure supply and therefore lower the risk for non supply | Routine/leverage items Aim: Reduce price by playing the market, possible outsourcing etc. |
|---|---|---|
| Quality | Secondary | Secondary |
| Quantity | Secondary | Secondary |
| Time | Number one | Secondary |
| Place | Secondary | Secondary |
| Cost | Secondary, maybe last | Number one |

On a cost/service and supply balance from the buyers/customers and demand perspective, then the following is indicated:

- Bottleneck/critical items have service requirements/KPIs first, especially the lead-time on delivery, with the cost KPIs secondary.
- Routine/leverage items have cost price requirement /KPIs first and the service aspects KPIs are secondary.

The matching response related to Kraljic, from the suppliers and supply perspective, is then going to be as follows:

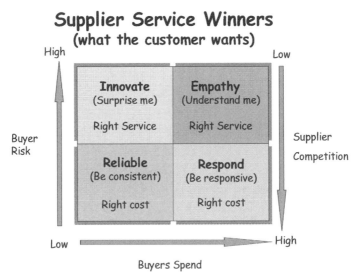

The above can be amplified further into an ideal-typical perspective as follows:

| Service Winner | Buyers Strategy | Matching Supplier Behaviour | Suppliers Market position |
|---|---|---|---|
| Responsive | Leverage items with Supplier Sourcing "Plays the market" | React rationally with price cuts | Certainty of Competition In the short and long term |
| Reliability | Routine items with Supplier Outsourcing "Organises and lets go" | React by exploring options and "fit" | Certainty of competition, in the short term, followed by stability in the long term |
| Innovative | Bottleneck items with Supplier Development "Secures supply and attempts to diversify" | Proactive entrepreneurial behaviour with new product designs, or, Reactive positions when maintaining the monopoly | Uncertainties of being able to innovate, high R&D costs, followed by possible monopolistic position |
| Empathetic | Critical items with Supplier Collaboration "Work collaboratively with suppliers" | Proactive team work and problem solving | Uncertainty initially (forming-storming) followed by long term performing |

The question to be asked here, is: Will the above-mentioned supplier behaviours line up with the buyer's strategy?

If there is congruence, there is agreement, and progress forward will be made as both buyer and supplier will have their needs met. If there is no congruence, then, whilst there are possible negotiations options, and positions may be changed, the outcome can be an eventual "no deal."

Clearly here, the appropriate behaviours by either party are affecting the supplier/buyer relationship. This is readily easy to accept (the "you get what you give" or and the "what you sow, you will reap" scenarios).

### Interpersonal behaviour in the supply chain
The above discussion also shows us the common and continuing organisational problem; the underpinning inter-personal behaviour of the people involved. These individual people being the suppliers /sellers/buyers/users and customers, who may actually do some things for their own reasons and not necessarily in line with what the employing organisation expects.

This is briefly explored below, and it will be seen that this can cause "interference", as what is actually going on may be different to what was expected or planned.

The leverage-buying and the responsive-supplying take us to towards transactional/adversary buying behaviours, that require a matching supplier behaviour of a rational response. The logical and stable thinking patterns revealed here are more of a logical left-brain approach. Providing this happens then there is good fit.

Routine buying and reliability supplying is also more toward transactional/adversary buying behaviour and requires as a service winner from suppliers, a response that explores options and is continually sensing for a "fit". The supplier is perhaps using exploratory and innovative

43

thinking patterns; a creative right-brain approach. This may conflict with the buyer's view of seeking a rational logical response. However, the supplier cannot give this, until they have explored creative options; a possible "no meeting of minds" here.

Bottleneck buying and innovative supplying leans more towards exploratory buying approaches, that requires service supply winners of intuition and exploration and eventual product change. This creativity also requires a more right brain supplier approach, and if buyers do approach suppliers this way, then there is a good fit. However, where the sellers wish to maintain any supply monopoly, they will now be displaying more rational and logical left brain behaviour.

Critical buying and empathetic supplying approaches require collaborative responses involving both logical thinking and emotional feelings; a typical combined right and left brain approach. This is difficult for many individuals to use and apply; hence a team approach can be used here to give a more effective balance with both logical and emotional traits introduced, and used as and when is appropriate.

Meanwhile, the following summarises these varied views:

| Buyers view | Buyer brain side | Seller brain side | Sellers view |
|---|---|---|---|
| Leverage | Left | Left | Responsive |
| Routine | Left | Right | Reliability |
| Bottleneck | Right | Right, but possible left | Innovative |
| Critical | Left and right | Left and right | Empathetic |

Clearly again here, whilst this is an ideal-typical model, one should appreciate the more appropriate brain sides that are needed and that "one size does not fit all". Approaches that recognise these varied and applicable options must be considered.

## Supply/Demand behaviour determines the supply chain

It is the outcome from the above buying/selling behaviours that will determine the resulting responsive behaviour of the physical supply chain. However, perhaps this is more difficult to initially see, so let us explain.

It is clear that demand drives the supply chain, as without it, there is no supply. Demand is therefore paramount and precedes supply. Suppliers offering an appropriate level of customer service to match the appropriate buyer's five rights will satisfy demand. This, as we have explained above, will vary hierarchically by the Kraljic categories. The suppliers' responsive appropriate level of customer service is therefore driven by the response to the customer demand and in turn, this is being driven by the buying behaviour of the customers.

What also are involved here are dependency, mutuality and possible variability, which are connected at the supplier/buyer interface. Dependency, variability and interfaces are all the "classic" aspects of all processes.

In offering a specific level of customer service, effective suppliers have segmented/categorised the customer's patterns of demand (for example, stable/unstable, fast/slow moving etc., all of these being more fully explained in *"Excellence in Inventory Management" (2007)*). This segmentation assists suppliers to plan their supply strategy, (e.g. make to order or make to stock), by which they are able to satisfy their customer requirements/needs.

Similarly, buyers will also need to segment or categorise suppliers. They may initially use Kraljic for their overall strategy, followed by options on specifying/sourcing, using vendor rating on supplier selection and the agreeing of the KPIs for the delivery/availability.

It is, therefore, the buyer's/customer demand that creates the design of the responding supply chain. Whilst "the customer is the business", the "supply chain is also the business". You cannot have one without the other.

As the requirements from suppliers and buyers differ, it follows that the format of the supply chain also differs. This will result in varied types of product supply chains.

### Types of Product Supply Chains
As we have noted, it is demand that triggers supply and therefore it is the customer/buying activity that will dictate the required supply. Essentially what is involved here is that the supplier, in order to meet the customer requirements, must obtain answers from the buyer/customer on the following questions:

- How much do you want? (Quantity-the demand driver).
- When do you want it? (Time-the supply driver).

Those aware of ordering and inventory management principles, will recognise the above parameters as the basis for the stock time curve.

An important aspect here for many buyers to understand, is that whilst they may place orders for a specific quantity, they are, too often, not very clear on the specific supplier lead-time. For example, buyers order 10 tons with a supplier's delivery in 10 to 12 weeks, but what really is it, 10 or 12 weeks? One wonders why the time is not made very specific; indeed it is extremely doubtful that buyers would order quantities of 10 to 12 tonnes? Why then agree to such variance on supplier's lead-time? It really makes no sense at all and will have an enormous impact to overall performance and to the inventory levels (this is again covered in *"Excellence in Inventory Management"* along with full explanations and options on managing the suppliers and the overall supply lead-times).

Meanwhile, the buyer's quantity/demand and time/supply aspects will in turn, give the following planning options for the supplier:

- The Demand drivers are either a definite order or a forecast. These will cover demand that is either, predictable or, unpredictable, (and hence, with the latter, the need to forecast) and result in, make to order or make to stock, production options.
- The Supply drivers are fast or slow product availability. These will cover the supply

of product that either has, already been made and is available ex stock or is, yet to be made/assembled to order. Therefore, the availability for the customer will be a shorter or a longer lead-time.

These demand quantities and supply times are planning options, and now give us four basic options, or types of product supply chains. These are illustrated below:

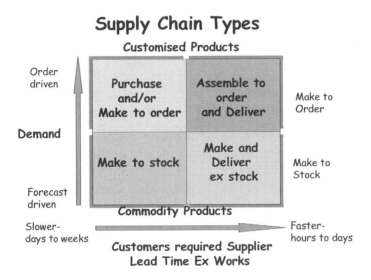

## Supply Chain Types

The lead-time has been shown as Ex-Works, this is for two reasons:

- The transit/delivery lead-time after the Ex-Works availability date will be very variable as it dependent on the distance (local to global) and the transport mode (such as road, sea, air).
- Whether the buyer or the supplier arranges the actual transit /delivery will be an option; this is not fixed and is an important buyer's choice and decision. Leaving suppliers to arrange delivery can disguise any Ex-Works or shipment delays that may only be revealed much later when buyers spend time expediting. This is too late and it is therefore much better to have had "real time" visibility of any delays. Knowledgeable buyers will therefore consider buying on an Ex-Works basis, as they then have the full visibility and track and trace on orders, and also have direct control of the freight costs.

The above demand/time matrix in turn, interacts with the actual supplied product volumes and the product variety, as seen in the following ideal-typical diagram opposite:

# Supply Chain Types

| | | | |
|---|---|---|---|
| Hi | **Purchase and/or Make to order** E.g. Some FMCG | **Assemble to order and Deliver** cars, computers | Mass Market Pull / Sell then Make |
| Lo | **Make to stock** E.g. steel, chemicals, | **Make and Deliver ex stock** most food | Mass Production Push / Make then Sell |

Product variety (vertical axis, Lo to Hi)

Hi ← Product Volume → Lo

Some words of explanation are needed on the "assemble to order and deliver" option and the "make and deliver ex-stock" option; these are where the customer requires a short lead-time and a fast response with quick availability.

**Make and deliver from stock:** (to meet demand, the customer needs a supply chain that is very responsive with a quick delivery. It must be noted here that the product is standard and is being supplied from stock).

An example of such a commodity product is some branded products that are supplied to supermarkets. Whilst a product like Heinz Baked Beans is a standard commodity product and is widely supplied to many customers, it can also require from some customers, a specialist and specifically designed agile or quick response (QR) supply chain. Whereas the demand patterns for such a product will be relatively stable over a longer time, the specific called-off and actual demand required "tomorrow," is not confirmed until a few hours (say 24 hours) before. Suppliers are then expected to respond. To do this, the suppliers must have detailed forecast systems, coupled with connectivity to the supermarket EPOS, so they may capture the real time demand. Indeed, with such connectivity, some suppliers may also become totally responsible for replenishments, delivering smaller orders on a more frequent basis, such as every day or by the hour. They will, however, only do this for some special customers, but will not do this for their entire customer base. The product is supplied from finished goods stocks that have been produced in high volume as a standard commodity, and are supplied to many customers who have varied supplier lead-times/service agreements.

**Assemble to order and then deliver:** (the customer requires a product that has some specialist characteristics and is made/assembled to order).

There are products that are required in hours/days and are supplied just in time (JIT). An example here is supermarket own-label carbonated drinks that are made/assembled to order, using a lead-time cycle of say, order end of day one, make/supplied during day two. Here, the product has some specialist characteristics, for example a bespoke label and product ingredients, and, therefore, such products cannot be supplied to anyone else.

Such customised products are also only going to be made to a specific order and therefore, stocks of finished goods are not going to be held in such a lean supply chain (so called as it holds no waste). However the lead-times can be longer than those for the 'make and deliver from stock' commodity products. For example, Dell computers accept a customised (or a bespoke order specification) and this order is assembled from stocks of parts/work in progress to meet that "unique" order. As it takes some time to do this, it will be supplied to customers in say 5/10 days.

**Implications**
The above types of product supply chain have many implications. For example, the key competences of a supplying manufacturing/production organisation is to be able to satisfy its customers' market demand, and the different ways it does this can be seen in the following ideal-typical diagram below:

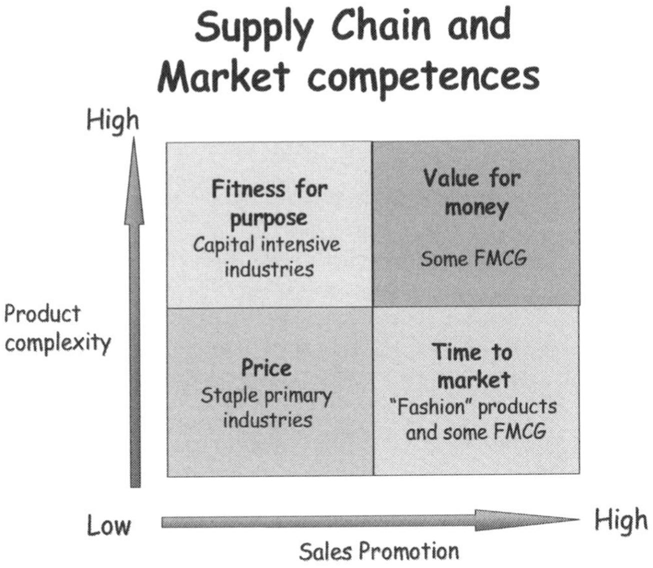

## Supply Chain and Market competences

We can develop these implications further by looking more at the effect that the "how much and when" questions/answers have. Taking the two dimensions of Make to order (predictable demand that is order driven) or Make to stock (unpredictable demand that is therefore forecast driven), we can see this actually gives five options; these are illustrated opposite and show where the format of stock is being held. The make to order options are shown in italics.

## Forecast or *Order* Driven Process

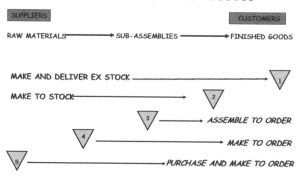

The above interactions generate some specific supplier requirements to meet the customer's needs. Looking at the two extremes of the forecast and order positions we can see the following implications:

| Activity | Make to Stock (1/2) Make then Sell Forecast "push" Supply-demand | Make to Order (4/5) Sell then Make Order "pull" Demand-supply |
|---|---|---|
| **Main Driver** | Forecasts. Structured planning and scheduling. | Orders. Sense and respond using real time information. |
| **Buying** | Is for anticipated needs and instructs suppliers. Focus is on cost and quality | Is for daily needs and uses involved suppliers. Focus is on speed, quality and flexibility. |
| **Product** | Standardised commodity products. Cost driven. | Bespoke and customised products. More quality driven. |
| **Supplier lead-time** | Fast and short as supplied ex stock | Slower as have to make/assemble |
| **Production** | Low cost with long production runs. High utilisation of plant. | Higher costs and short runs with fast changes. Uses excess buffer capacity. |
| **Inventory** | Cost is in finished goods with safety stock. Stock is seen as an asset and a protection. | Cost is in raw materials and work in progress with little safety stocks. Stock is viewed as a liability. |
| **Distribution** | Storage costs are high with low transport costs (product is being moved in bulk) | Storage costs are low with high transport costs (product is moving in smaller quantities and more frequently) |

The previous table may appear relatively straightforward, but it is already getting complex as it generates some wide-ranging options and implications. These, however, get even deeper; consider the following Type I and Type II supply chain contrast.

**Type I and Type II Supply chains: A contrast**
The following ideal-typical model for two types of supply chain extends the above view and also presents an "extremes" view to stimulate debate and discussion about the differences and the changes that may be needed.

This is not intended to be a "good" or "bad" comparison, as the reality and the practice will be found in the "grey" between the "black/white" extremes; also, some aspects can be mixed between the two types. For example Type I on the main drivers and products; but Type II on inventory and buying etc.

| Attribute | Type I Supply Chain<br>Production led<br>Product push<br>Make to Stock<br>More about supply | Type II Supply Chain<br>Market led<br>Order pull<br>Make to Order<br>More about demand |
|---|---|---|
| Main driver | Forecast driven.<br>Growth from volume output and ROI.<br>Financial performance profit driven.<br>"Pump" push.<br>From Supply to demand.<br>Mass production. | Order driven.<br>Growth from customer satisfaction.<br>Customer focus, value driven.<br><br>"Turn on the Tap" pull.<br>From demand to supply.<br>Mass market. |
| Products | Launched.<br>Functional, standard, commodities.<br>Low variety.<br>Long product life cycle. | Transition.<br>Innovative, design and build, fashion goods.<br>Higher variety.<br>Short product life cycles. |
| Inventory | "Turns."<br>Stock holding.<br>Just in case.<br>Hold safety stock.<br>Seen as an asset/protection. | "Spins."<br>Little stock holding.<br>Just in time.<br>No safety stock.<br>Seen as a liability. |
| "Buying" | Buy goods for anticipated and projected demand/ needs.<br>Instructed suppliers.<br>Arms length, played off on a short term basis.<br>Confrontation.<br>Adversarial.<br>Narrow range of suppliers.<br><br>Low cost buying.<br>Inspection on receipt. | Assign capacity on a daily basis.<br>Involved suppliers.<br>Committed suppliers, long term.<br><br><br>Cooperation.<br>Alliances.<br>Ordered supplier base of specialists.<br>Total acquisition cost buying.<br>Quality assured. |

| "Making" | "Build." Proactive with orders. Economy of scale. Continuous flow and mass production. Long runs. Low production costs. High work in progress inventory. High plant efficiency e.g. 24/7. Labour is an extension of the machine. Ordered "push" schedules and reliable demand forecasts/make to stock. | "Supply." React to orders. Reduce waste. Batch, job shop, project methods of production, "customising". Short runs. Higher production costs. Low work in progress inventory. High effectiveness but with lower plant efficiencies. Labour brings the continuous improvements. Flexible "pull" Kanban schedules with make/assemble to order. |
|---|---|---|
| "Moving" | Move slower in bulk. Large/less frequent deliveries. Storage is high cost. Transport is a low cost. Fewer but larger RDC type deliveries. | Move faster in smaller quantities. Smaller, frequent deliveries. Storage is low cost. Transport costs are higher. Many varied and dispersed destinations. |
| Customers | Predictive demand. Cost driven. Are only handled at the top or by the "customer service" department. | Un-predictive demand. Availability driven. Everybody is customer focussed. |
| Information | Demand information is sometimes passed back. Used mainly for "executing". | Demand information is mandatory. Used also for planning purposes. |
| Handling of Customer orders | 10% forecast error and algorithmic based forecasts. Continuous scheduled replenishment. More "push". Stock outs rarer (1-2%) and are dealt with contractually. Stable and consistent orders, some predictable weekly type ordering. Clear cut ordering. Service levels are more rigid. | 40-100% error with forecasts more consultative based. Real time visibility throughout the supply chain. More "pull." Stock outs are immediate and frequent (10-40% p.a.), volatile. Cyclical demand, many unpredictable orders. EDI/Visibility ordering. Service levels are more flexible to actual forecasts. |
| Deliver from stock lead times | Immediate, fast in one or two days. | Immediate to long; slower and from days to weeks. |
| Make to order lead times | 1-6 months as mainly making "standard" products for stock. | 1-14 days. |

| Costs | Mainly in physical conversion/movements. Inventory costs in finished goods. | Mainly in marketing. Inventory costs in raw materials/WIP. |
|---|---|---|
|  | Cost control very strong and any gained savings are retained. | Revenue generation and any gained savings are shared. |
| **Producer selling price** | Low selling price. Few markdowns. 5-20% profits. Low risk. | Higher selling price. Many end of season markdowns. 20-60% profits. Higher risk levels. |
| **Organisation methods** | Silo/hierarchical management with some "cells". "Top down" to staff gives orders and responsibility. | Flatter structures with cross functional teams. Top down and bottom up giving assistance; everyone is responsible. |
|  | Professional managers who are more driven by power. Transactional/ownership. Self interest. Protective interfacing links. Slow to change, change is mainly resisted, and maintenance of the "status quo". Internal fragmentation with instructed employees. Tendency for "blame" cultures. "Fire-fighting" Little trust. People a liability and numbers are to be reduced wherever possible. Narrow skill base. Outside recruitment. "Do what you are told" | Leaders/educators who are people driven. Partnership/collaborative. Customer interest. Visible integrated links. Quicker response with continuous improvement and more embracive of change. "Joined up" structures with involved employees. More "gain" structure. "Fire-fighting" Extensive trust. People are an asset to be invested in. Multiple skill bases. Internal recruitment "Do what you think is best" |

**Demand and Supplier management**

Demand is important; it has different characteristics and drives the supply chain that suppliers will have to respond to. As shown above, these resulting supply chain processes will also then differ conceptually.

For buyers to ensure that demand is going to be adequately satisfied, the supplier must be managed consciously. This supplier management cannot be left to chance or left with any unconscious power plays.

Suppliers are connected to customers, and the supplier input clearly affects the customer's output.

The total performance output is also going to be dependent on the supplier's inputs and the intervening supply chain processes that are used.

# Part one: Summary

- Procurement is one part on an integrated supply chain that connects suppliers and customers.
- Procurement can be handled differently and structurally by organisations.
- Kraljic provides a valid view of such differences in the procurement process by examining risk and spend. Accordingly "one size does not fit all".
- The procurement cycle shows procurement is a process that goes across and through organisational departments. We specifically looked at in part one, the pre-order stage.
- The 5 rights of procurement (quality, quantity, time, place and price) clearly show the connections between suppliers and customers and also provide the key performance indicators for both parties to use.
- The connection and interface between suppliers and customers/users must be managed for mutual value creation. Supplier Management and Supplier Service are names that can be used to do this.
- Supply/Demand behaviour determines the supply chain by defining how the "how much and when" (the demand quantity and the supply time) aspects will be dealt with.
- As the demand and supply differ and vary, this means that there are different types of supply chain with different processes within these supply chains.

# Part Two: Supplier Management – The Supplier's View

We mentioned in part 1.0 the procurement cycle and discussed the Pre-order stage. After this pre-order stage, the following is involved:

**The Order stage:** Ordering – Progressing/Expediting - Delivery/receipt

**The Post order stage:** Payment /Invoice verification – Reviewing

These stages have been already fully covered in our book *"Excellence in Procurement" (2008)* so this detail will not be fully covered here. However, to highlight specific aspects for supplier management purposes, we will briefly mention here those relevant aspects from the Order and Post order stage.

## Handling orders and Progressing and Delivery

If all appropriate agreements have been made, including organisation and agreed supplier lead-times, then, providing the buyer/customer has fulfilled their part of the bargain, it can be reasonably accepted that the supplier will also complete their part of the contract. It will also be expected here that appropriate KPIs have been agreed with suppliers to effectively monitor that the 5 Rights are happening as was expected. We will talk more about this in part 3.0.

Accordingly, it should not be necessary to spend time progressing and expediting orders. However, for one-off purchases where there is no history or record of supplier performance, some progressing and checking may be required to ensure suppliers meet their contractual agreements. It can also be widely used for critical items required, for example, in oil and gas production, and also where there are no proper arrangements or collaborative supply thinking.

For Global Sourcing there is a relatively simple way to better control Import Supply Chains and to expedite proactively. Importing involves a more distant supplier with extended transit lead-times. As lead-times are used in making calculations, and key components in deciding how much to order from suppliers, the knowledge and control of lead-times is critical.

However, what often happens is that a decision is taken to import on CIF or C&F Incoterms and, therefore, the buying importing company has left the organisation of the transit with the suppliers. Effectively, then, the control of the associated lead-time is also externalised. thus. importing organisations often have to spend time expediting and checking where the goods are and when they will arrive.

Delays in transit times can also cause potential product shortages, with impacts to customer service levels and not satisfying their requirements. When there are regular repeat orders, then delayed transit times will inevitably add to increasing stock holding, as the buying company will need to hold stocks to protect against the uncertainty of the suppliers lead-time.

It is however possible to better control the imports by switching to Ex-works (EXW) or Free on Board (FOB) Incoterms.

By doing this the following potential benefits may be realised:

- Control and knowledge of exactly what is happening; management needs to recall here that the management cycle not only involves planning, organising, directing but also controlling.
- Visibility and knowledge of exactly where the products are during the transit; as simply, the transit it is now in your control.
- Cheaper freight costs as you are now directly paying them; importers and buyers need to really believe that suppliers are more than likely to have a margin on the actual freight costs they have paid. Even where the freight costs are shown as a separate item above the FOB price, then you will rarely find that anyone has checked on the validity of these charges.

A useful place to start is to understand some of the aspects of total supply chain management, for example:

- What are your costs of holding inventory?
- What supply lead-time is required
- What part of the supply lead-time, is the transit lead-time?
- What are the effects of reliable and consistent on time in full receipts and how does this compare to your current situation?

Answers to these questions are always revealing and often show how the internal structure is fragmented and effectively unorganised to undertake effective importing. Answers will also provide the basis for accessing the benefits of changing.

The next steps are as follows:

- Ask for the suppliers EXW price.
- Negotiate freight terms, possibly by going out to tender or having better market knowledge of freight costs. For example, costs can also fall and at the time of writing, (mid 2008), the general freight cost from the Far East to Europe have fallen from USD 1200 to USD 800 per TEU, purely due to competition in the freight marketplace.
- Check on the track/trace system to be used. This can be a simple key point reporting with spreadsheet recording, or, an instant on demand access to a carriers system.
- Assess the risk of changing, for example, possibly extra management costs, insurance covers and freight variation rate exposures. It is important to ensure a like-for-like comparison with the current methods as many of the current costs may well be hidden, for example, the insurance and freight increase costs are currently being paid

for in the existing CIF terms.
- Compare and contrast
- If deciding to change, and effectively changing the buying strategy, please ensure that the internal structure supports the changes.

There is much evidence to support that the changes detailed above are worthwhile, as the following case studies show.

## Case Study: A major food retailers - Imports

Spend was £1200 million on imports via third party wholesalers and £500 million on direct imports. For example, home and leisure products were ordered through UK agents who arranged everything to DDP. Meanwhile, beers, wines and spirits were bought EXW works or FOB with freight arranged through various forwarders. A change in management identified that they had:

- no systems
- no cost visibility
- no economy of scale
- poor product availability
- an internal fragmented structure; for example, trading on product selection, negotiations, selection of suppliers, and ordering; finance on letters of credit, payments; logistics on order quantity and phasing into supply chain

The company tendered and then outsourced to one forwarder, but maintained and determined carrier selection when appropriate. The results were:

- Freight costs fell by 8 per cent
- Duty charges reduced by 10 per cent
- Fuller visibility of supply chain
- Reduced stock levels
- Centralised the previous fragmented internal control as a new structure followed the new strategy

## Case Study: A major clothes retailer - Imports

Had nearly 200 stores had 70% of products imported, mainly from Far East. They identified that they had the following problems:

- No accurate data therefore no visibility
- Orders arrive "unexpectedly"
- 40% time spent of phoning/checking
- Paid high demurrage/rent port costs
- Restricted on buying currency forward
- Poor QC

The solution was to:

- Change from C&F to FOB and use one UK forwarder
- Set up a simple database tracking on transfer points. PO, confirmed, tariff heading, cargo booked, authorise shipment, confirmed shipment, documents banked, documents received, arrival time, clearance time, arrival at DC, QC checked, released/available.
- Integrated all their internal systems

The benefits reported were:

- Lower demurrage costs
- Improved warehouse efficiency due to scheduled arrivals
- Improved finance due to forward currency buying
- Quicker customs clearances
- Better product availability

## Case Study: A supplier of cleaning products - Imports

Supplies branded products to major retailers and cash and carries, along with own-label products to a number of the leading retailers. Cost-cutting initiatives had become a way of life in the face of major supply chain challenges. The company's supply chain manager noted that: "In the past four or five years we have had to work hard at controlling our costs at a time when there have been no price increases from our customers".

The operation therefore changed to buying products Ex-Works. The challenge of bringing in consignments cost-effectively is made more difficult by the low-value nature of the products, many of which are very light and use up large quantities of space. The organisation's success is seen as directly related to its freight cost management and arrangements.

**Payment**

On an individual order basis, the payment to suppliers needs to be completed. This will be in accordance with contract agreements following from earlier negotiations. Payment terms are often a major aspect of the supplier appraising and evaluation steps and are certainly very important to suppliers; especially those (most) of them, who are in private commercial sector where cash flow is a major concern to an organisations survival. Longer payment terms will invariably mean one of two things, the supplier goes out of business, or the supplier covers this cost from their profit margins in the quoted/negotiated price.

Delayed and late payments are a source of friction between suppliers/ customers; they may also be in breach of contract terms. The handling of any payment complaints from suppliers must also involve the supplier relationship holder; it is really not acceptable for organisations departments to always direct supplier payment queries to the finance department. Supplier performance is important and not being paid on time in accordance with agreements, will be a major source of discontent and can ultimately lead to changes in the supplier's performance and, ultimately, their withdrawal/resignation.

### Reviewing

The market in which an organisation competes and the products it provides will be part of its business strategy. This will define what goods will need to be sourced to satisfy market demand; this will in turn provide the basis for the supplier and procurement strategy. The sources to be used are then identified by buyers in order to meet these strategic decisions. The amount of reviewing, monitoring and control allocated to an agreement will, therefore, depend upon the importance of the product or service being procured, in relation to the business strategy. *"Excellence in Procurement" (2008)* covers such price reviews, procurement costs, total organisation spend and risk factors.

## Suppliers have needs

As we have just noted, information has to be gathered on the market conditions, as the available options for sourcing will be affected by the product or service being sourced and the availability, location, number of suppliers and competing buyers along with the market growth.

From a supplier management perspective, we must also consider the satisfaction of need; the starting point for procurement from the users/customers perspective. As we have already suggested earlier, this is actually a "two-way street", as suppliers are also looking to have their needs satisfied.

A buyer's ability to influence a supplier to do something is largely dependent on the buyer's perception of the supplier's willingness to meet the buyer's need. The opposite is also true, where a buyer's ability to influence a supplier is also dependent on the supplier's perception of the buyer's willingness to help the supplier met their needs. Finding ways to ensure both parties' needs are satisfied is therefore an issue to be considered and as we have already partly examined earlier, this will influence the behaviour patterns between buyers and suppliers.

Firstly, let us consider the balance of power between suppliers and buyers.

### Power and Kraljic

Supplier management will also be influenced by the relative power of buyers and sellers. Therefore, the power of each party also has a part to play; an overview of this is provided overleaf:

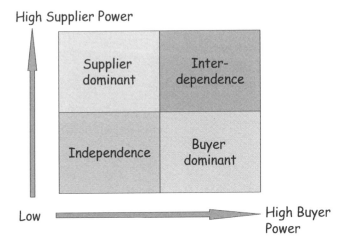

High Supplier Power

|  |  |
|---|---|
| Supplier dominant | Inter-dependence |
| Independence | Buyer dominant |

Low → High Buyer Power

Power is not going to be equally distributed, and the relationship with Kraljic and procurement strategy can be seen as follows:

1)      Buyers are dominant on **Leverage items** as there are many competing suppliers of standard commodity goods that the buyer purchases in large volumes. Therefore, this is an attractive proposition to those suppliers who see attractiveness in volume sales at low price. Buyers can easily exploit their buying advantage by "playing the market." When the buyer is dominant we will find:

- A small number of big buyers with a large market share and a high spend and influence
- They buy a large percentage of a seller's output
- It is easy for the buyer to switch suppliers, creating a "take it or leave it" view from the buyer
- There are many sources of supply giving a highly competitive supplier market
- Low transaction costs

2)      Suppliers are, however, dominant on **Bottleneck items**, as they have a bespoke product, often branded, which the buyer has to purchase; so buyers must ensure and secure supply, whilst searching for alternatives. When suppliers are dominant we tend to find:

- A small number of big sellers
- Supplying to many buyers
- Difficult for buyers to switch
- Few sources of supply as suppliers have "unique" products. For example, OEM spare parts
- High transaction costs
- An "enforced" view from the supplier

- There are barriers to entry for other suppliers into their market, for example, requirements for specialised research and development

3) Buyers and suppliers are interdependent on **Critical items** where for example, alliances enable sharing and collaborative working for mutual benefit

4) Buyers and suppliers are however independent on **Routine items** as minimal effort is needed for sourcing these items due to the relatively little impact procurement can make to reducing costs. Buyers thus look for reliable and efficient supply and, once this is found, they can "let it go", for example, the outsourcing of stationery supplies to just one supplier with whom those, who need stationery, will make direct contact to place an order.

It cannot be assumed by buyers that every supplier is "desperate" to supply them with products or services; indeed this may only occur with Leverage items and even then, with the low price on offer, some suppliers may not be interested in the business.

**Power and Economics**
The type of market and its association to power exists in economics, as can be seen below:

| Aspect | Monopoly markets | Oligopoly markets | "Perfect" competition markets |
|---|---|---|---|
| Supply & Demand Control | Statutory controls and checks exist in the UK | Fewer organisations, with the possibility of market collusions | Few controls, most things are open |
| Barriers to entry | Retained and suppliers look to maintain the "status quo". | High costs to enter the market for any "new" suppliers. | Few to no barriers of entry with low costs to enter. |
| Market view | Focus and concentrate. | Large and valuable markets. Possible cartels. | Customers can easily "switch." Continual customer searching for a better deal. |
| Customers view | Not really considered, as the customer has no choice. | Sometimes considered, possible competition between suppliers. | Customer "rules" and drives the market. |
| Prices | Can charge "what the market will bear." | Stable and related to costs and desired profits. Possible price fixing. | Demand driven, possible cost plus provision. |
| Arguable Examples | Oil production, although some alternatives do exist | 4 UK Supermarkets control over 60% of consumers spend, but there is some competition | Consumer goods for example, cars, electronics. |

**Supplier's views**
Suppliers will have also have a view of their market and this will affect a supplier's positioning towards their customer's buyers, for example (see overleaf):

**Source: Steele and Court (1996)**

So for example, suppliers may be seen as exploiting when they are the sole providers of a buyer's bottleneck item. Suppliers may also view some buyers as a nuisance when the buyer is seen to be very demanding and unreasonable.

Clearly then, not every customer is going to be seen by the supplier as being a key account or a "core customer".

In turn, we can see that the supplier's objectives may be as follows:

# Suppliers Objectives

| | |
|---|---|
| **Development** Expand business | **Key Account** |
| | **Exploit** Premium price |

**Supplier's and buyer's views**

For effective supplier relationships, the above 4 supplier's objectives can be matched to the earlier 4 Kraljic buyer's objectives. This gives rise to 16 options, so let us start by looking at leverage items and see how this fits with the above supplier's objectives

# Suppliers & Leverage Items

| | |
|---|---|
| **Development**<br>Supplier development.<br>Encourage<br>Participation. | **Key Account** |
| | **Exploit**<br>Adversarial-both<br>chasing profit.<br>Stimulate<br>Competition. |

With a buyer's routine items, again the key account and development objectives of suppliers enable a good match for both parties; with the other two options require buyers to seek alternatives.

# Suppliers & Bottleneck Items

| | |
|---|---|
| **Development**<br>Potential risk.<br>Raise mutual<br>dependency. | **Key Account** |
| | **Exploit**<br>Cost risk.<br>Monitor service.<br>Change supplier. |

With critical items we find buyers needing to seek competition, with a potential match requiring closer working for the development supplier's objectives, whereas the key account objective clearly fits.

### Getting the best from suppliers

What happens therefore when a buyer is not actually a key account of a supplier?
The question from the above analysis shows the following two options:

- Change the suppliers. This is clearly a risk for bottleneck items and will also involve the subsequent time spent in searching, sourcing and evaluation.
- Develop the suppliers. This is fine as long as the supplier also has this as their objective.

Efforts can be appropriately directed, including of course, efforts to find and encourage those suppliers who see the buyer as a key account. However, having suppliers who see buyers as a key account will not automatically happen. Indeed, as the above simple analysis shows, this will only happen in 4 out of the 16 permutations.

Therefore, asking, finding and searching for the true reality of how a supplier views you is important. This must go beyond asking just say the salesman, who may be be somewhat biased.

Honest conversations between the right people are needed: *"whilst the Supply Chain is driven by flows of materials, information and money, it also needs people working together in flow - that special state when people are connected and think together; when we have a positive relationship with no separation; when we have connected our hearts and minds. Only then, can we realise supply chain success."*
**(Source:** Emmett. *SAPICS.* 2007)

The only way to find out what suppliers think of you is to ask them how happy they are; just as we would normally do with customers. The following survey methods may therefore be considered

1) Face to face/ telephone
- Ask open questions = expansive answers
- Tell me = ask directly
2) Questionnaires/ hard copy/electronic/web based
- Yes/No/rate on 1-5 point scales
- Rate also against the competition

Questions to ask suppliers:
- How often do we do things right the first time?
- How often do we do things right on time?
- How quickly do we respond to your requests?
- Do we keep commitments we have made?
- Do we pay you on time?

- How accessible are we when you need to contact us?
- How helpful and polite are we?
- How well do we speak your language?
- How hard do you think we work at keeping you a satisfied supplier?
- How much confidence do you have in us?
- Overall, how would you rate how we compare to others you supply?
- How willing would you be to recommend us?

Many buyers will be surprised by responses to such questions. Some buyers are actually "staggered" when they find out they are not being viewed as core customers. The writers have many times experienced a buyer's surprise when a supplier has told them that they no longer wish to deal with them and that their business is no longer important to the supplier. However, as it becomes more important for buyers to be a supplier's customer of choice, the days of endlessly playing one supplier off with another are ending for some buyers. Indeed, a survey of buyers has reported that:

*"72% believe becoming a customer of choice will be important in the future"* and continues, *"As long as procurement demonstrates professional and ethical behaviour then suppliers are more likely to engage with them. Follow this with fair contracts and incentives and you will be top of their list of favourite clients."*
(**Souce:** *Supply Management 27 March 2008*; Power and control.)

Additionally, a few aspects about working better together may be helpful:

## Some Lessons from Experience

### 1.0. The case for it
*"The only way forward is to get players working to a common agenda – the collaboration agenda. We have been taught to compete: nobody has taught us to work together. The need and awareness is there but still nobody has taught us how to do it".*
(**Source:** Professor Alan Waller)

### 2.0. Some things to consider:
- *"Personal relationships that bridge former gaps in communications between vendor and retailer are what can really spell success".*
- *"It changes the paradigm. It's definitely a different type of relationship with your customer. It's based on mutual trust and it's got to be there to succeed".*
- *"On paper, the process seems simple to implement, but in the real world of personalities and professional relationships, there are many obstacles to climb. Trust is very important for success".*
- *"You have to interested in being criticised".*

### 3.0. The benefits found:
*"Benefits of our Collaboration programme include:*
- *Improved service levels.*
- *Faster flow of product through the supply chain.*

- *Rational use of resources and more effective promotion planning.*
- *Synchronisation of production to better match supply with demand.*
- *Shared responsibility and mutual trust".*

**(Source:** FMCG Retailer and Supplier)

*"A real focus on joint and collaborative planning has been critical. It's all very well putting in great capability and structurally changing our supply chain but at the end of the day you can't make it happen unless you work together."*
**(Source:** *Logistics Manager June 2004*)

*"Key suppliers work collaboratively, ensuring efficient processing and best practices, driving our competitive edge".*
**(Source:** *IBE Report 2006*)

**Behaviour**

The above supplier relationship approaches will very likely require a behavioural change; indeed some observers readily note that supplier relationship management is really all about 70-80% behavioural change and only 20-30 % process change. Additionally, in January 2007, one procurement manager, when asked for his predictions for 5 years forward said, that then his job title would be relationship manager.

However, there may be much to do here, especially when comments like the following are reported:

*"The Mail on Sunday alleges the Retailer was asking 700 of its suppliers for a contribution from their contracts and the company was to lengthen its payments terms from 60 to 90 days".*
**Supply Management 18 January 2007**

*"The Company is locked in a bitter dispute battle with its suppliers over attempts to extract cost savings from its supply chain...One supplier claimed the company were arrogantly out of touch."*
**Sunday Times 11 February 2007**

In both of these reports, it would seem the buying organisations have suppliers of leverage items, as they are displaying buyer power, which has been interpreted by one supplier as arrogance.

Another description of behaviour, between buyers and suppliers, is revealed by the following examples of sales and buyers evaluating each other.

What a supplier needs from buyers can be seen by the traits of a good buyer, as seen by salespeople. These are as follows:

- Does not act aloof towards the seller.
- Does not try to get a lower price to be used as leverage against the existing current supplier.

- Assists in contacting appropriate people in their company when they find they lack knowledge or authority. They also explain the buying process in their company.
- Allows adequate time for a presentation.
- Has a working knowledge of their company's products.
- Maintains good credit standing and pays invoices promptly.
- Have good relations with their company's top management.
- Follows ethical procurement practices.

From this it would appear that a poor buyer is one who is aloof and arrogant, is secretive about internal contacts, hurries presentations, has poor knowledge of their company, and does not pay promptly.

A good supplier can be seen by the traits of a good salesperson from the buyer's perspective. These are as follows:
- Offers a thorough presentation and a good follow through.
- Has a good working knowledge of their product line.
- Is willing to go "into bat" for the buyer within the suppliers company.
- Shows knowledge of the market and a willingness to keep the buyer informed.
- Has a good working knowledge of the buyer's product lines.
- Uses imagination in applying their products to the buyer's needs.
- Uses diplomacy in dealing with operating departments.
- Follows ethical sales procurement practices.
- Prepares well.

From this it would appear that a poor supplier is one who is not thorough or prepared well, has poor knowledge of their own company, will not look after buyers interests in their own company, has poor knowledge of the market and the buyer's products, is not diplomatic when dealing with other departments in the buyer's organisation and uses unethical sales techniques.

Using the above lists to measure or view the actual behaviours can be revealing. This will indicate what actually does take place, and perhaps lead us to conclude that the following style of negotiation and discussion are preferable:

- Participants have a problem solving approach, where wise outcomes are reached, amicably and efficiently.
- Separation of the people from the problem, by being soft on the people but hard on the problem.
- Exploring and focusing on interests and not on positions.
- Avoiding having a bottom line.
- Developing options for mutual gain.
- Insisting as far as possible on objective criteria.
- Listening and being open to reasons.
- Yielding to principles and not to pressure.

Behaviour displayed during meeting, discussions and negotiations, will most definitely affect all of the parties involved. Consider the following comparison on negotiation behaviour styles:

| Adversary negotiation style | Collaborative negotiation style |
|---|---|
| Compliant supplier | Partner supplier |
| Supplier is unsure of the buyer's or customer's/user's real needs | Work together to agree needs and the means to satisfy them |
| Supplier maybe closed and hostile | Supplier is open and friendly |
| Cold contractual issues are discussed | Warm and "how to improve" issues are discussed |
| Each side tries to minimise risks for themselves | Risks and prevention measures are explored |
| Each side tries to pass risks onto the other | Sharing of risks is allocated by agreement |
| Each side tries to score off the other | Each side tries to find benefits |
| No risk taking, growth or development | Innovation and assured quality with expansion and growth |

The inevitable win-lose adversary style will, however, often be defended as being appropriate, as this prevents the other side from attacking them first (what was called, by the British Lions Rugby team in the 1970s, as getting your retaliation in first). We seem also to be back here to Professor Alan Waller's view that we have been taught to compete and not to cooperate. There is also the expression that you get what you give, therefore non-cooperation will in turn bring about non-cooperation.

It seems paradoxical that people consciously reflect their own concerns and do not anticipate this behaviour pattern will be shown back to them; this may be done covertly or be remembered until "pay back time" in the future.

The reality can also be, therefore, that, whilst people will recognise that trust is needed between suppliers and buyers/customers, they will actually exhibit a lack of trust. Well-known expressions elicit the following: what you see is what you get, and that people believe what you, actually say or do, and not what you say you want to do.

Such behaviour patterns can also occur outside of negotiations and be displayed in normal communications; behaviour continues beyond negotiations and a specific pattern emerges. Often this may be framed by the procurement strategy and/or, by the individual personalities of influential people. This behaviour will, therefore, impact and influence the responses received from suppliers.

Such responses from supplier's can also affect the prices quoted to buyers; please consider the following:

## Exercise: Suppliers Pricing

Imagine you are a supplier; not a buyer and that your company has a good reputation for supplying high-end specialist IT services to a specific market sector. You have a history of supplying the two major customers in this market sector. At the moment you are not supplying either of them. They are both large and important and look good on your customer list. They provide you with a good springboard for more business with other customers in the same market.

Almost at the same time they both ask you to quote for a new project with the same specification for each one. At present you do not have the capacity to supply them

69

both. Your average quote-to-sale conversion rate is typically one in three. So you decide, on this occasion, to quote for both jobs and pull out of one if the other gives you the go-ahead. This is not an unreasonable strategy since, with a conversion rate of one in three you might not get either of the projects, and there is only a one in nine chance that both will say yes.

### Customer A
- Likeable people who are enjoyable to work with
- Prompt payers
- Give clear specifications
- Demanding
- Set very high standards
- They regularly visit to check what you are doing
- They understand your problems and often sit down with you to help sort them out
- They demand fast service, sometimes quicker than you can provide
- They are open to explanation if you have genuine reasons for failing to meet their deadlines
- In short, they are your preferred customer; a joy to work with.

### Customer B
- Some likeable individuals with whom you get on well
- They are poor payers - sometimes invoices are 'lost', and occasionally they have taken 90 days to pay
- Different departments contact you separately, often with different messages
- No one function seems to be in overall control
- They keep changing the specifications
- On the last contract you thought you had provided exactly what was required, but they weren't happy and forced you to make changes free of charge
- They are unhelpful, don't like answering questions and rarely return calls.

### The Project
- Cost of £400,000 in time and materials
- You normally add 10% contingency to cover unforeseen charges, taking the cost to £440,000
- Then you usually add a 10% profit margin, taking the cost to £484,000
- Finally, on goes a bit more to allow for negotiation after the quote has gone in.

The size of that 'bit more' is up to you.

### Task
As the supplier, decide what you are actually going to quote to customer A and customer B to win the business. Think about it carefully as the way you think, and the decisions you make will be very instructive.

(**Source:** After Will Parsons, www.qualitair.co.uk)

In playing this exercise "live", inevitably the lower price goes to customer A, the one who is "tough but fair". Meanwhile, customer B gets the higher price as they show poor behaviour, is a poor payer, sometimes loses invoices, occasionally takes 90 days to pay up, has different departments/different messages, keeps changing specifications etc.

The facts are clear, customers who treat suppliers poorly, will pay a price. Regrettably, many suppliers do not realise this and remain with their own perception – one that lacks empathy. This single-sided view can also happen with leverage items. Here, any poor buyer behaviour will also impact on suppliers and may negatively affect the buyer. This surprises some buyers, perhaps understandably, as leverage items do represent buyer power; so let's explore this more fully.

### Behaviour and power on leverage items - a special word

Suppliers do have the choice to refuse orders for commodity leverage-based work from some customers, for example those like customer B above who pay poorly, delay payments, change specifications and requirements at short notice, do not provide updates on changes etc. However, such customers are often negatively upset when such shortcomings are pointed out to them. They may then rationalise the comments as "you are the only one", "take it or leave it" and "no one else has a problem" etc.

The reality, however, is that the buyer's behaviour does, more than likely, actually cause these others to have a problem, but these others have chosen to "keep their heads down" and in so doing, have blocked any chances of open communication and continuous improvement between what could be cooperating players, who are aiming for their own versions of "win/win".

Often, the view here from buyers with leverage items, is there is always someone who can do it cheaper, and that perhaps doing things better is maybe not needed, or at worst, is not even considered.

From the supplier's perspective, "putting their head about the wall", when they are viewed as a leverage item, may be seen as a risky strategy for them to use. When the supplier has the customer as a core or key account, then maybe they see it is best to keep their head down and practice a negative form of compliance. However, they then effectively camouflage any chances for improvement in their customer's organisation; effectively a "win/lose" that is, however, invisible to the customer!

Conversely, where suppliers of leverage items have just the one customer, or where a customer accounts for a significant part of their turnover, some forward-looking buyers do realistically appreciate this can be dangerous for both parties. It also can lead to having suppliers who are submissively compliant and display non-challenging, negative and passive behaviour.

In this regard, Miles Davis, jazzman *extraordinaire*, once noted that he preferred to play with musicians who challenged him, as he got something extra from them that changed and improved what he did.

Challenging is important for change and improvement, please see the following checklist:

## Checklist: Change and Challenging

This involves conflict and compliance; however these words can be easily misunderstood. To give clarity therefore, we have explained below the positive and negative sides of both conflict and compliance.

- **Positive conflict**

This is constructive as it enables new learning through an open disagreement and discussion on ideas between people. The outcome is either a full agreement about the others position, (there has been a "We" view and a "walking in each others shoes"); or, finding a new "third" position, this is through taking an emotional detachment and an objective "helicopter view". All those involved believe they have gained something from the conflict process.

- **Negative conflict**

This is destructive as it inhibits new learning through creating personal tensions among people. The outcome is on "one" position only; "I", which sees this "own" view only. The position taken is essentially founded on an emotional subjective response. Those involved are usually divided, as whilst one may feel they have gained, the other feels they have lost something.

- **Positive compliance**

This open challenging encourages positive conflicts and recognises these are needed for effective learning and changing. People are actively involved in shaping the outcome from a mutual awareness and understanding of the differences. They can change their position in the process.

- **Negative compliance**

This encourages blind or forced agreement, which hinders effective learning and changing. It is effectively closed challenging as it discourages any open challenge and positive conflict on any differences from the *status quo*. One party remains uninvolved and keeps quiet with "unspoken disagreement". This gives a "false" agreement, which can encourage mistakes to be repeated, and little change brought to the *status quo*. People will internally remain with their own position, even thought this will not be externally expressed in their "false" agreement.

Meanwhile those organisations that choose to ignore supplier-suggested improvements and therefore refuse to consider change, may then find they continually have a fast rate of "supplier churn" (which may be costly to them), but it will also likely lead to stagnation in the medium term and therefore bring them a very visible "lose".

Those that choose to listen and discuss, will gain and "win". A parallel here can be drawn about managing and handling one's own employees and two questions can be asked of our behaviour in these circumstances:

1.     *"Is the "stick" or the "carrot" used when we manage our people?"*

2.     *"Which of these, over time, gives us the best results?"*

For the writers, the answers to these two questions are so clear that this leads us to ask: why should our behaviour with suppliers be any different, so that we can then get the best from suppliers?

Why some buyers ignore such simplicity is frankly, most amazing. Many organisations must therefore remember that they are only as good as their suppliers. Additionally, in times of increasing outsourcing, supplier relational management becomes "mission critical." After all, what comes in to an organisation does eventually create what goes out; the "rubbish in-rubbish-out" analogy. This means therefore that relationships with suppliers need managing effectively, if they are not, the very business itself may be at risk.

### Behavioural understanding and meeting needs
It is increasingly the view of many observers that behavioural understanding is going to be increasingly important in Suppler Management.  For example, "the (London Heathrow) T5 contract took technical competence for granted and focussed as much on the behavioural competence of both organisations and people".
(**Source:** Riley, *"Flying in Formation"* in *Supply Management 13 March 2008.*)

Building trust, respect and integrity is vital for a sustainable deal, but knowing how to achieve this, without being seen as weak, and without being exploited, is not always going to be easy or straight forward. We will explore this further in part 5.0 of this book.

Monitoring relationships and the ensuing performance is therefore critical, as shown in the following case study:

## Case study: Philips

Philips is a global operator in the electronics market with factories all over the world. In order to compete and to ensure customer satisfaction, Philips has to manage its quality and procurement strategy very carefully. The company recognises that customer satisfaction depends on the quality of what happens on the production line, which in turn depends on the performance of suppliers. If any of the links in the chain break down or fail to meet the required standard, then all the glossy advertising in the world is not going to make up for the customer's disappointment in a product that is unavailable, or does not work properly, or fails to meet their technical expectations.

Total quality, therefore, is an ingrained philosophy throughout Philips' operations, resulting in better products and better processes. 'Philips Quality' has five simple, but important principles:
(a) Strive for excellence
(b) Customer first

(c) Demonstrate leadership
(d) Value people
(e) Supplier partnership

Directly or indirectly, many of these principles could not be properly implemented without good relationships with the right suppliers. Philips cultivates supplier relationships based on trust and co-operation, sharing experience and expertise to benefit not only the buyer and the supplier, but also the end customer. Together, Philips and its suppliers develop technology, solve problems, learn from experience and try to avoid errors and misunderstandings.

Clearly, Philips cannot develop and maintain deep relationships with every one of its suppliers. Instead, it assesses its suppliers to discover which ones are the most important in terms of their strategic significance to Philips' business. These receive the most attention and investment in relationship building. Philips has three categories of supplier:

1. Supplier-partners: this might be the smallest group, but these are the most important suppliers and Philips builds intense, involved relationships with them. An important focus of the co-operation is innovation, the development of new expertise and new opportunities. These suppliers might well have essential knowledge and/or expertise that Philips could not otherwise access or develop for itself. This makes these suppliers extremely significant strategically as their loss could seriously undermine Philips' current business and future direction.

2. Preferred suppliers: these suppliers are less important, but there is still good reason for Philips to work closely with them on issues such as quality, logistics and price to gain mutual benefit. The supplier does adapt itself to suit Philips' requirements, to some extent, but there is not the same mutual dependence as in the first category.

3. Commercial suppliers: these are the least important suppliers and although Philips will encourage better performance in terms of quality etc., it is unlikely to get involved in helping the supplier to achieve it.

Philips also emphasises the importance of supplier revaluation as a basis for improving future performance. A supplier's actual performance is measured against mutually agreed targets in terms of quality, logistics, costs and responsiveness.

Behavioural and cultural understanding must also include mutual understanding and empathy, which leads to a level of satisfaction between suppliers and customers.

As the following diagram shows, there can be varied positions found in the satisfaction of needs between suppliers and customers.

# Supplier / Customer Satisfaction

| Position | Suppliers perception | Customers perception | Action needed |
|---|---|---|---|
| Success | Satisfied | Satisfied | Build/develop on these strengths and look for new ventures together |
| Satisfaction/ Dissatisfaction | Satisfied | Dissatisfied | Discuss issues and determine corrective actions needed |
| Dissatisfaction/ Satisfaction | Dissatisfied | Satisfied | Discuss issues and determine corrective actions needed |
| Separate | Dissatisfied | Dissatisfied | Negotiate out of any deal, part and say goodbye. |

Where dissatisfaction occurs, understanding about the other parties' supply chains and organisation is likely to be missing, and poor communication will often be found. Communication must therefore be regularly "health checked" and examined; the following questions may be considered:

- Are there any agreed clear milestones/review points?
- After every meeting/communication, did we agree the time/pace for the next one?
- Do we record by email but use also the phone, (as this gives intimacy/personal communication)?
- Do we have regular face-to-face meetings?
- Do we separate the person from the problem?
- If we clash, is this on ideas and not on personalities?
- Do we work on interests not positions where we try to satisfy the underlying need and not the stated position?
- Do we generate a range of options and work towards a shared search and evaluation of solutions that uses measurable objective criteria?

75

Poor communication will virtually and systematically always lead to poor results. Indeed, communication must, itself, be a budget item in supplier management. It needs to be costed with an appropriate time allocated. The cost can be calculated on a simple basis related to either the contract time (for example, at a ratio of 1 day to 10 days), or by spend (e.g. at 10% of spend).

The main point here is that the effective management of suppliers does, of course, cost and must therefore be budgeted for. Whilst there is a cost associated with doing this, there are certainly higher costs if this is not done. For example, a comparison before the successful construction of London Heathrow Terminal 5, found that the average outturn contract performance for similar projects, was an overruns of 40% on time and 15-23% on spend. These are enormous extra unanticipated costs involved that can be avoided by taking appropriate steps. Supplier management is one these steps.

At the beginning of this part of the book we noted that the buyer's ability to influence a supplier to do something is largely dependent on the buyer's perception of the supplier's willingness to meet the buyers need. The opposite however is also true where a buyer's ability to influence a supplier is also dependent on the supplier's perception of the buyer's willingness to help the supplier met their needs.

Finding ways to ensure both parties' needs are satisfied is therefore an issue to be considered, for, as we have seen, this will influence the behaviour patterns between buyers and suppliers.

# Part two: Summary

- The procurement cycle post order was examined.
- Both buyers and suppliers look for their needs to be satisfied.
- Buyer Power, Kraljic and Economic Market positions were examined.
- Suppliers also have views on these positions and these views were compared to Kraljic buyer's views.
- Where there are mismatches between these views, then honest conversations are needed, in this regard, then managing supplier relationships is likely to involve 70/80% behavioural change and 20/30% process change.
- Buyers and suppliers do have preferred views of each other and behaviour is shown during the negotiations and contacts.
- The varied levels of need satisfaction between suppliers and buyers/ customer were compared and noted that suppliers also have a perception of how buyers can help suppliers to satisfy the supplier's own needs.

# Part three: Supplier Relationship Management

## Definition

Supplier Relationship Management (SRM) is the management of the whole interface between supply and buying organisations through the whole life of the contract. The aim is to achieve maximum long-term contribution from the supplier that works towards achieving the buying organisation's strategic goals.

The key differentiator from conventional contract management is the focus on the whole interface with the supplier. This may cut across many contracts and SRM therefore concentrates on the supplier contributing towards the buyer's long-term strategic goals.

## Benefits of SRM

Developments such as outsourcing and strategic partnering have increased the size and the importance of the contribution that suppliers can make. Up front or pre-contracting activities are still very important, but the initial signed contract is only one part of the whole. As a supplier's operation becomes more and more integral to the organisation, then all of the activities around the management of the contract and the management of the supplier become critical. It is also the positive supplier relationships that will produce any sustainable competitive advantage.

Indeed, the authors suggest that for complex purchases, most of the value obtained from the supplier is actually going to be driven by post contract management, rather than from, the up front negotiated contractual terms.

Additionally, as procurement rationalises the supply base and reduces supplier numbers, then those suppliers who remain, become more powerful. Therefore, if the relationships with these fewer, stronger suppliers are not managed properly, this may present a risk to the business.

As was discussed earlier, being the "customer of choice" is increasingly important, and the better the relations, the more likely they will be that customer of choice. This becomes particularly important if is a seller's market.

*"You have to be attractive otherwise if there's a bigger partner, the supplier will go with them."*

One of the most persuasive arguments for SRM comes from Henke (J Henke, Oakland University) who believes that he and his team are on the edge of directly correlating strong supplier relations to a percentage difference in prices, so that if organisations go about SRM correctly, they can insist on more from their suppliers.

*"If they do it the right way you can put more price cut and improvement demands on suppliers. If organisations can guarantee business and suppliers know you will support them when things go wrong, and work with them to improve things until you can't anymore, then suppliers will stick with you, not just switch allegiances."*

An example here is Phillips:

## Case Study – Philips Electronics

The company has selected 30 strategic suppliers, a move which has reduced the time to market of some goods by 50 per cent, i.e. twice as fast.

They had two suppliers of a particular product, one of which was running out of capacity so needed a third, but they didn't really want to do this because of Intellectual Property rights issues.

So they sat down with their two suppliers, each from different backgrounds and agreed to work together to improve productivity.

SRM can therefore lead to cheaper prices, gives faster time to market, has more flexibility and brings in innovation.

### Taking the lead

Many commentators see that it is actually up to the procurement department to determine the nature of the supplier relationship. The argument used here takes the view, that suppliers may not always decide what sort of relationship they will have with buyers/customers and that suppliers will only be able to react to the way buyers/procurement behaves towards them. This point of view is also reinforced by our assertion above in Part 2.0, that it is the buyer's demands that actually result in and create the type of supply chain.

After accepting the need to do this leading, then the "two coming together" are now able to later blend better, learn from each other and synergise; consider the example of L'Oreal below:

## Case Study – L'Oreal

L'Oreal procurement has been building long-term relationships with suppliers for the past few years to support growth. Their approach is based on mutual respect, transparency and sharing information.

### How are the existing relationships?

Once buyers have identified whom to work with using SRM principles, then measuring the health of the existing relationship is the next stage. It will be necessary here to identify:

- Where the supplier relations are.
- Where you want the supplier relations to be.
- The status of your supplier relations, in absolute terms, across different sectors, sizes, countries.
- How your perception compares to that of your suppliers.

**Starting out**
The key components that drive SRM are trust, communication, whether you can help the supplier (e.g. to improve cost and quality), whether you hinder the supplier (e.g. by making late and excessive changes) and finally for a supplier, what opportunity they have to make a profit.

## Checklist: Critical success factors for starting SRM

- A management mandate to make sure your company wants to do SRM
- Build SRM approaches into sourcing methodologies by not only creating SRM manager roles but also by educating and training staff on SRM approaches
- Supplier relationship managers need adequate skills and passion.
- Establish the required behavioural norms
- Manage the stakeholders.
- Look for increased and incremental value over the duration of contracts and relationships
- Build joint working forums focused on identifying and delivering joint improvement programmes
- Incentivise and reward suppliers to deliver demonstrated value
- Focus on total cost of ownership (TCO) and life cycle costs where any increased price can be evidenced and supported as a positive outcome as the TCO costs are reduced.
- Realise quick wins to motivate and work towards creating long term value
- Establish mutual interest and relation targets
- Performance needs to be measured, as only what is measured gets done. So have joint targets for the relationship that will, for example, increase productivity or mitigate risk.
- Don't wait for the right time to start; this will never happen, so just start.

At least once a year the major stakeholders of the two buying and selling organisations should meet. At these sessions they should seek to understand each other's intentions, priorities, exploit common ground and deal with any problems. They conclude by agreeing common goals and setting an action plan.

## Checklist: Critical success factors to consider when managing SRM

- Remember you buy from individuals, not organisations
- Be open and fast in your communication with suppliers – there's nothing worse than trying to hide bad news

- Building trust takes time and effort
- Try to maintain a "full reservoir of goodwill" because you never know when you might need to call in a favour
- Procurement managers/directors would be better to see themselves as Relationship managers/ directors

## SRM Case Study approaches

## Case Study – BP

BP believes SRM programmes require about 70 percent behavioural change and 30 percent process adjustment.

First the company segmented its suppliers to decide where to concentrate its efforts. It examined assurance and compliance to check if it was getting what it should from current deals, looked at spend volume and the value of the deals it had in place, and also examined what suppliers thought. It did this with the help of Honda, Toyota and an independent survey.

Of BP's 51,000 suppliers, it discovered it had just 6 to 8 key strategic suppliers. The next tier "sector critical relationships", had around 170 suppliers, and there are around 800 with whom BP has sector and/or local relationships.

Its SRM and supplier performance management programme – aimed at these groups – is expected to net savings of $200 million. Start slowly with process based decisions around supplier performance until trust is established. "If you have been beating them up for the past few years, it will take you at least 24 to 36 months to get them to talk about relationship management."

Buyers had to send clear and consistent messages to suppliers and set KPIs appropriate to the relationship. For example, with top targets around innovation measurement for only the tier one supplier.

KPIs should support the organisation's overall objectives and performance management. Clear strategic goals, the right contracts, effective planning and capable managers should all be in place.

## Case study – AVIVA Financial Services

"It reduces total cost of ownership and creates competitive advantage through deeper relationships with suppliers. For example, it means you may get privileged access to innovation, the best people, products and services within the supplier organisation."

## Case Study – McDonalds

SRM helped the organisation focus on long term relationship needs and that it enhanced communication and helped to prevent "relationship value degradation". It also creates greater visibility, access to supplier capabilities and fosters innovation.

## Case Study – British Airways

"You need to get the supplier to internalise you so that you become their "customer of choice". The world is currently moving into a world of scarcity, particularly because of the growth of India and China. The biggest challenge is competing with other buyers, not necessarily getting suppliers to compete."

## Case Study: Philips' Procurement Strategy

The initial selection of suppliers is an important strategic decision and an essential stage in the procurement process. Both the supplier selection process and the assessment criteria have been defined.

The selection process consists of:

- Identifying the strategic products
- Identifying potential suppliers
- Assessing and selecting suppliers
- Defining the relationship with selected suppliers

After following this selection process it becomes possible to define the type of supplier relationship, identifying those that have a strategic impact on the overall business. Assessment criteria are:

- Business capability (technological, manufacturing, commercial, logistics
- Availability of products and services
- Avoidance of conflict of interest
- Management structure and company culture
- Required confidentiality
- Financial position

In addition, the supplier's quality assurance system must be in compliance with the relevant standard of the ISO 9000 series and be certified by an accredited third party.

### Relationships with Suppliers

As a leading electronics company, Philips are very involved in developments in electronic technology. Such developments have a considerable impact on the design of products, which require increasingly tougher specifications. Success in these fields depends on close working relationships with suppliers. These require the development of supplier-partners on a 1:1 basis, the strategic importance of the relationship being underlined by top management involvement in the procurement process.

While good relationships are sought with all suppliers, intense working relationships can only be maintained with a limited number of suppliers. In order to identify the optimal supplier base, suppliers are classified into categories which determine the level of relationship.

The three categories, in increasing level of involvement are:

- Commercial suppliers
- Preferred suppliers
- Supplier-partners

### Commercial suppliers
Philips seeks to maintain and continuously improve product quality, delivery conditions and cost without specific initiatives from Philips' side.

### Preferred suppliers
Mutual objectives have been identified and acknowledged by both parties. The preferred status is reciprocal. Philips has a preferred customer status with the supplier. The supplier introduces and implements TQM principles with Philips' support (if needed). Both strive for improved performance in quality, logistics and price.

### Supplier-partners
In this closer relationship, in addition to sharing present expertise, supplier-partners co-operate in building new expertise and developing new business opportunities. The supplier-partner has, for example, fundamental proprietary knowledge which Philips must draw upon in order to launch a new range of products. The number of supplier-partners will always be quite small because this mutual dependency only exists for a small number of products. The strategic importance of the supplier-partner relationship is underlined by the involvement of top management.

It is to Philips' advantage to involve suppliers with a specific expertise in the product creation process from the start. Such expertise must, of course, have been demonstrated by the quality of the supplier's previous products and processes. Early cooperation makes it possible to utilise suppliers' knowledge and skills optimally and forms the basis for a short development time and timely introduction in the market. Sharing expertise is also the best way to control costs, both in the development stage and in the manufacturing process.

To reinforce the alliance with a supplier-partner, a senior manager (not necessarily from procurement) is assigned to act as the supplier's advocate. It is the task of this advocate to facilitate communication between the two organisations, remove managerial barriers, and make it possible, for example, to exchange planned developments in technology.

The boundaries for procurement processes are, to a great extent, determined during the product creation process. To reach a balanced decision on the specification of materials and the required supplier capabilities, the voice of all primary functions must be heard at the earliest possible stage.

A multi-disciplinary team comprising representatives from procurement, development, product management, and manufacturing brings together the competence for making the best decisions on product quality, logistic aspects, costs and supplier selection. Such teams provide the interface for early supplier involvement. Subsequently these teams provide the context in which supplier partnership can flourish and become the base for continued cooperation across functional boundaries.

It would be short sighted to evaluate a supplier (and thus the performance of a purchaser) on the basis of negotiated invoice prices along. Other cost factors, such as transport, product quality, lead-time and stock obviously determine the cost as well. Total cost of ownership takes all these factors into account.

Open calculations and ship-to-line programmes can help to eliminate avoidable costs of ownership. Philips will support improvement programmes aimed at controlling processes at the supplier's end. This will cut down on avoidable costs and thus crate a "win-win" situation for both the supplier and Philips alike.

An integral requirement of every improvement programme is to upgrade the performance of the supplier in product specification, product quality, timely delivery and total costs. In each area targets are set and actual supplier performance is rated against mutually agreed upon targets. This systematic rating brings objectivity and focus for improvement. Minimum parameters on which suppliers are systematically rated are quality, logistics, price and responsiveness.

The basics of the rating system remain the same, notwithstanding differences between division and business units.
The objectives of supplier ratings are to:

- Check the supplier's performance against the mutual target;
- Foster a continuously improvement process;
- Acquire the basic information for supplier assessment';
- Evaluate the relationship with a supplier.

# Case Study - Chrysler

Car manufacturer Daimler-Chrysler is to spend an extra £2.5 billion on sourcing from low cost countries. The organisation also plans to reduce the cost of the materials it uses by £773 million. The organisation will rely "more heavily on leveraging partnerships to manage costs", including working closely with suppliers to develop more cost effective products.

## Case Study: Research into SRM

Organisations across a variety of industries are reporting difficulty in managing their suppliers, according to a study by Archstone Consulting.

While many organisations have conducted strategic sourcing and outsourcing to reduce costs, few have mastered SRM as a critical part of enhancing their supply chain and reducing overall costs.

Organisations that lack SRM elements such as supplier governance, performance management and supplier development, are often unable to realise the full value of their supply base.

A total 58% of respondents reported an inability to hold suppliers accountable and ineffective use of incentives and penalties. Fewer than 10% said current systems can effectively support SRM.

The research found that while most SRM initiatives are in their early stages, organisations have achieved or expect to achieve significant benefits. These include a 7 – 11 percent reduction in cost of delivery and a 10 – 14 percent reduction in procurement headcount.

## Case Study: Research into SRM Leaders

Organisations that invest in supplier relationship management achieve greater savings and respond more quickly to changes in the marketplace.

The study by Accenture found that leaders in SRM achieve savings of 3 percent on their annual procurement spend, whereas other organisations achieved only 1 per cent.

The study classed organisations that achieved more than 50 percent of procurement benefits from post contract award activities as "SRM Leaders". Most leaders were found in the media/entertainment, car and pharmaceutical/health industries, with property/facilities management, banking/insurance and manufacturing having fewest.

Whilst the majority of organisations expect the future focus on SRM to increase; there is a shortage of staff with relevant expertise.

# Case Study – Automotive Industry

Attempts by Ford and General Motors to improve supplier relationships "may be starting to work" research has found.

The Original Equipment Manufacturer (OEM) – Tier 1 supplier working relations annual study found that while Toyota and Honda still have the lead in good supplier relations and are the preferred carmakers in the US to do business with, efforts by Ford and General Motors seem to be working. The principle reason for this is that both Ford and General Motors are providing more timely and adequate information to suppliers than had been done in previous years.

The improved communication leads to greater trust, both of which are important components of strong working relations

# Case Study – Asda

"Drilling down" appears to be a vital aspect of successful SRM and supplier collaboration and integration was an area that Asda was quick to home in on when it turned its attention to sourcing from local suppliers.

The supermarket now has a dedicated local sourcing team whose sole aim is to identify local products and work with small suppliers to enable their products to reach the stores. The team enlists the support of regional food groups, customers and colleagues to discover essential local brands in each area and decides which stores they would sell in. If there is large demand for a product, they ensure the supplier is not overwhelmed and work together to reach supply agreements.

"Local products often come from very small suppliers," an Asda spokesperson says. "Therefore it is important for us to make it as cheap, easy and risk free as possible for these suppliers to do business with us. This means we have had to change the way work."

Reduced payment terms have been introduced to help ease cash flow problems and no costly technology is needed. Unlike other suppliers, local vendors do not need an electronic information system that processes and receives orders and payments. A simple fax will do the job.

Each local supplier is given a glossary and guide on how to complete necessary paperwork, which has been simplified with the jargon stripped out. Goods can also be delivered direct to the store.

A food hygiene accreditation system has been created between Asda's technical team and an independent lab. "It is just as effective but simpler, quicker and cheaper to implement than the current industry standard," the spokesperson says.

**Closer Connections**

In addition, supplier days are regularly held to bring all Asda's local suppliers together. This not only fixes teething problems, but ensures they have access to as many members of Asda's local sourcing team as possible. The supermarket has also drawn up a commitment to the supplier. This includes selling products for between three and six months regardless of sales figures to give the product every opportunity to succeed.

## The role of procurement departments

Many organisations are not capitalising on the benefits of supplier relationship management; despite the beneficial evidence referred to above.

An Accenture survey analysed data from 229 senior procurement executives from a range of industries in 13 countries. It revealed organisations that actively managed suppliers were able to respond quickly to marketplace changes, reach customers with the "right priced products and services" and, ultimately, optimise the value delivered through the relationships over their lifecycle.

Procurement departments, the survey concluded, can deliver real benefits to a company when they work cross-functionally with other departments and suppliers. Despite the findings, there seems to be little consensus as to which organisations should approach SRM and, indeed, the role procurement departments should play in it.

One important finding was that few organisations have actually developed well-structured, comprehensive approaches to SRM.

A study of soft supplier management related issues by Polychronakis and Syntetos (2006), explored the interface between the suppliers' organisational culture and structure. They, not surprisingly, concluded that certain combinations of leadership styles will facilitate or hinder supply chain integration. They found that adversarial approaches by buyers displayed a lack of commitment to long-term business and here was a complete absence of two-way communication, trust and an arms length interface. An essential condition for effective supplier development therefore, was the extent to which an organisations culture facilitates the proactive co-ordination of activities between partners. Appropriate support structures can lead to positive efforts for supplier development, longer-term contracts and sharing of information.

Organisations are now realising, they need to actively manage suppliers and contracts, as part of long-term strategic category management. They can then deliver and demonstrate the savings and benefits promised through their sourcing and negotiating process.

SRM requires a medium to long-term strategy, a comprehensive set of tactics, approaches and tools, supported by structured and frequent management of all aspects of the supply agreement and supplier relationship. This is explored further in Part 4.0 of this book.

**SRM needs a new skill set and outlook**

British Airways and others have observed that the skills buyers are traditionally trained in are not the same, as those skills required for traditional procurement activities. SRM requires a longer-term perspective and the use of a range of soft skills; this is not always easy for logical minded numbers driven people; for as has been said, it is the soft skills that are actually the hard skills in business.

The following checklist indicates more on the SRM skills and approaches needed:

## Checklist: The SRM Skill set for Managers

Supplier relationship management demands an intricate blend of hard and soft skills.

Traditional procurement is focused on "doing the deal", whereas SRM has a broader remit on the long term health and value of the supply relationship. To be effective, SRM requires an intricate blend of the following soft and hard skills.

- Communication. The ability to communicate effectively through a variety of channels, internally and externally.
- Interpersonal sensitivity. The ability to understand the other party's point of view.
- Negotiation. The ability to influence internal stakeholders and the supplier in relation to objectives, and to manage conflict.
- Project management. The ability to manage the processes and promises of delivery by both the supplier and the buying organisation.
- Technical. The ability to measure, monitor and cultivate the relationship through tools such as balanced scorecards and continuous improvement programmes.

## Case Study: Research into leaders in SRM

SRM leaders have done the following:

- Supplier segmentation; identifying the right buyer-supplier relationship to form part of the strategic sourcing process.
- Contract management; enabling comparative analysis and the monitoring of contract compliance.
- Supplier performance management; the monitoring of suppliers' operational, administrative and cost management performance.
- Integration and collaboration; integration relates to systems integration with key suppliers, allowing for more streamlined planning and fulfilment. Collaboration relates to joint improvement planning.
- Correct organisational structure: where SRM is a critical function and the cross-functional team efforts are institutionalised and encouraged.
- The right people whose skills are developed and deployed: with a focus on working more closely with key suppliers to deliver value over time, for both the supplier and their own organisations.

- The right technology to capture and assimilate supplier specific information and data.

## Case Study: Centrica

Centrica have brought together the two functions of Procurement and Supplier Relationship Management into one department in recognition of the importance of laying the groundwork for effective long-term contracts.

## Case Study: BA

BA developed a three-pronged SRM strategy because many of its supplier relationships are complex and long term. The strategy involves a "Category Management planning process" where BA works out which suppliers it can "relationship manage" – the airline spends on average, UKP 3.80 billion a year and aims to actively manage 80 percent of that total.

Of the cost benefits they report, 60 percent comes from supplier management activity.

Once it has identified who to manage, an account plan is drawn up outlining what BA wants to achieve with the supplier. It states:

- who is in control of the relationship
- potential risks
- details the supplier's interests

The airline researches how well the supplier is performing via online surveys and looks at buyer satisfaction and supplier responsiveness.

The final aspect is an Internet-based systems tool for buyers. It provides answers to problems they are trying to solve, suggests what path they should take, who should be involved and how they can get to where they want to be.

BA believes that contracts are very important but they do not describe the whole trading relationship. Procurement departments tend to focus on doing deals. This is important, but misses the point. A big part of what procurement should be doing is managing the supplier, to bring in more sustainable advantages.

Procurement once thought information translated into power, but today realise that the power is in the sharing of information, which in this context, provides an opportunity to reduce costs that can be shared by all the constituents within the supply chain.

As we have mentioned many times, too many organisations believe that the management of the procurement process actuality stops at the placing order stage and then the procurement department moves on to the next negotiation/the next deal, leaving the contract to manage itself.

This is an area that needs to be addressed, particularly as organisations are becoming more global and where sourcing and outsourcing has become increasingly reliant on an extended supply chains. As this trend continues, the need to actively manage suppliers and performance becomes even greater.

*"Global procurement functions are doing well in terms of their visibility and cost cutting efforts, but poorly on contract management."*
(**Source:** Ariba Live Conference 2005)

*"Major barriers are the lack of internal competency to manage partners".*
(**Source:** PTRM 2007; *Global Supply Chain Trends 2008-2010*)

With increased competition in the market, organisations will need their suppliers to provide sources of value and differentiation. If an organisation fails to manage its supplier relationships, it is then leaving to chance the realisation of any potential latent value in the relationship.

## Effective Supplier Relationship Management

Effective SRM can deliver value for the organisation through a solid sourcing process and supplier management approach that will lock in the value from sourcing, this being so often lost in the post contract interactions. It can then extend the value delivered from suppliers through an ongoing focus on collaboration and integrations.

The need for the management of a supplier after the "deal" has been concluded is therefore fundamental, so that organisations are able to achieve the real benefits from their procurement strategies.

It is not good enough for organisations to draft a first class agreement with a top supplier and then simply sit back and expect the medium to long-term benefits to roll in. In a world where expectations and performance standards are always getting higher, organisations need to be able to build and maintain relationships with their major suppliers if they are to capture the maximum long-term value from the supply chain links and connections.

Supplier management provides this catalyst for organisations to acquire products or services that will meet or exceed their expectations and to give them competitive advantage.

However, it need not be restricted to the post contractual phase of supplier relationships. Effective management of suppliers during the sourcing and contracting process will normally produce a much better result, as here the buyer can then better and clearly communicate their expectations and in turn, require and demand, a greater insight into a supplier's infrastructure and capabilities. Indeed we will examine this aspect further by a case study of 3PL (third party logistics) service provision selection in part 6.0 of this book.

Relationship segmentation is a critical element in planning a supplier management programme. As discussed earlier, approaches to supplier relationships will differ depending on the difficulty of the market in which the buyer is operating, the anticipated duration of the relationship or, the perceived probability of further engagement between the parties. This is shown below in the Supplier Management Behaviours diagram:

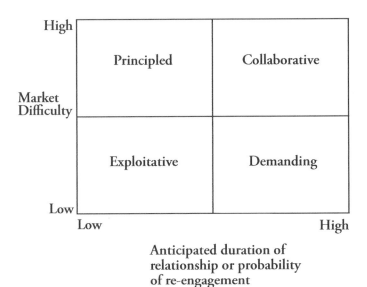

**After:** Johnson, R, 2003

Many organisations do actually remain too "deal-focused" and are not good at all in managing relationships. Effective supplier relationship management will provides an integrated communication and information driven management process and one that is clear to all those who have the contact with suppliers.

To put supplier relationship management in context, the following diagram provides an overview of the whole Supply Management process, which illustrates how the objectives of any supplier management policy can be derived from the sourcing strategy.

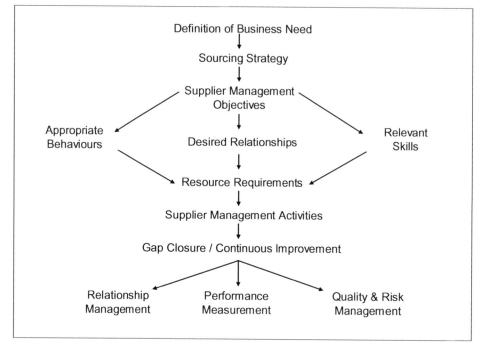

As with any process, and procurement and supplier management are no exception, they need to have an iterative element. Such a review process will result in regular feedback, enabling the organisation to better determine their continuing business needs and supplier management objectives.

In an effective supplier management process, suppliers will come to expect a higher level of meaningful feedback to help them improve their operations at all levels. Feedback from their customers will typically include regular reviews and analyses of areas for improvement.

Effective supplier relationship management can then provide suppliers with the necessary opportunities for improvement through a process of regular measurement, review and feedback. Where necessary, it can also help suppliers to develop the capabilities to meet current and potential customer needs, enabling them to drive out costs and inefficiencies throughout their own supply chain that will benefit both parties.

## Contract Management by Non-Procurement people

Sometimes non-buyers in organisations have to get involved with the ongoing contract management; the best approach to use is the following three-step process:

1.  **Educate** non-buyers so they know what it means to manage a contract. This is the most empowering step as it gives them the insight to understand the ramifications of their contract management decisions.

2.   **Enable** the non-buyer with tools and processes and support their knowledge by offering a framework in which they can apply this newfound knowledge.

3.   **Support requirements**, this is the most strategic step and there are two options here. Procurement people agree to serve as an adviser or they become the lead contract manager. Either of these options will strengthen the relationship between buyers and the non buyer as by leading contract management activities, procurement will free up the non buyer to concentrate on their direct responsibilities. By agreeing to serve as an advisor on contract management activities, this then leaves buyers more time to develop value adding procurement initiatives.

Good contract management does not necessarily rely solely and only on procurement experience, but rather on having effective managerial, negotiation and interpersonal skills.

It is important to clearly define the scope of the respective roles, for example, who handles contract reviews, performance management, cost reduction activity and contingency planning.

Training should be provided on these and other basic principles, and ongoing advice and support for specific contract issues including relationship management, risk management and terms and conditions. Procurement support should also be given for key review meetings, negotiations and dispute resolutions utilising contract review templates.

## Case Study: Bank of England

Non-buyers should take charge of contract management, according to the former head of procurement at the Bank of England.

Deals that perform well are often neglected, for example one healthcare contract, had not been looked at for seven years because it delivered good service. However by them working more closely with the supplier, significant savings were made and the level of service was also increased.

One way of tackling this neglect was to devolve the management of contracts and suppliers to those departments that have the expertise in that specific area. HR staff could then manage the healthcare deals or the executive team could be given responsibility for existing consultancy contracts because they know what is expected of suppliers.

## Case Study: Research

Most purchasers believe non-buyers are capable of handling contract management. According to a "Supplier Management" poll of 100 buyers, 78 percent agreed non-buyers should, at least sometimes, handle ongoing contract management.

It was agreed that it is procurement's role to equip non-practitioners with the training, tools and support that allows them to manage contracts more effectively.

## Balanced Scorecard Management System

The balanced scorecard (BSC) enables organisations to clarify their vision and strategy and translate them into action. It provides feedback around both the internal business processes and external outcomes in order to continuously improve strategic performance and results.

If Supplier Relationship Management (SRM) is to be successful it is necessary for organisations to implement a formalised, structured approach to measurement and therefore the balanced scorecard approach can be of value. The balanced scorecard management system is essentially a performance measurement process, as shown by the following diagram.

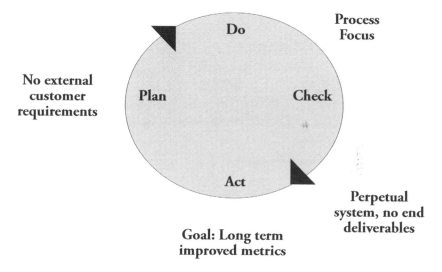

The BSC process, derived from Deming's Total Quality Management, is a continuous cyclical process. It has neither a beginning nor an end.

SRM is a process which endeavours to gain added value from suppliers by striving for continuous improvements in total costs, innovation and service levels and therefore relies on such an approach.

## Case study: BP Egypt

BP has a scorecard for Well-Testing Services
*   Traditionally, once a contractor has passed the minimum requirements at the technical stage, they were then chosen on the lowest price criterion at the commercial stage.

- One of the consequences of this was that over time, it was noticed that there were gaps between the standards expected by BP from the contractor's staff, and the actual performances provided.
- An analysis of the situation found that there were gaps between expected skills and competency levels and the actual levels of the staff being supplied on the contracts.
- Following a benchmarking exercise with BP Trinidad, BP Egypt devised a Skills Assessment Model.
- This sets down the levels to be provided by the contractors and measures actual skill levels against these standards to identify gaps.
- Clearly it was necessary to agree the standards, as well as for both sides to agree the existing levels of skills for the staff on the contracts
- Contractors were asked to measure the skills themselves and BP would then measure and agree a mutually acceptable level.

The following areas were measured:

Experience     45% weighting
Interpersonal 20%
HSE             15%
Technical       20%

Each of the above area was broken down into skill definitions and both sides assessed each one according to the levels below:

0 = no experience in the assessed area
1 = basic
2 = competent
3 = highly competent

Once gaps in skills had been identified, a joint action plan was agreed to develop the skills to the required level. As a result, skill levels improved and performance overall as a consequence ensuring:

- lower total costs
- less downtime
- higher efficiency and effectiveness

Obviously such a Skills Assessment Model has to be continually applied to ensure continuous improvement. Following the successful introduction into the Well Testing Services function it is intended to roll–out the model to other services and will be embedded into any future supplier appraisal and selection process.

**Shaer, S.E (2008)**

As we have just seen in the above case study, BSC involves three essential skills, as shown below.

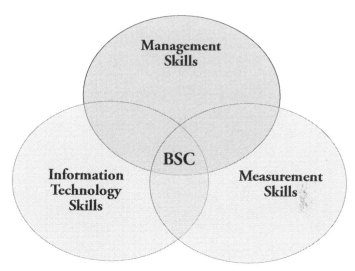

The basic idea is to focus the organisation on metrics that matter from a strategic Supplier Management point of view. To avoid focusing only on short-term financial measures, the scorecard therefore uses metrics from areas such as the customer, internal processes and interestingly, a learning and growth perspective. BSC is essentially therefore the process of translating strategy into action by turning the company's strategic vision into clear and understandable objectives. These can be communicated to and shared with the suppliers.

In the financial perspective of the Balance Scorecard, focus is on how the company should position itself to be considered an attractive and exciting investment to its owners. To achieve these financial objectives the company will have to bring some kind of value to its customers (the value proposition) that the customer considers to be higher than the price paid.

In order to achieve those customer objectives the company will have to excel at certain internal processes. These objectives are described in the internal processes perspective.

Finally, in order to excel at these processes, the company has to provide an infrastructure and the necessary human capital to pull it off. These issues are being addressed in the learning and growth perspective.

Once you have decided on the objectives within each of the perspectives, it is time to sort them into "themes" of objectives that belong together in a cause and effect relationship. These themes form the basis of communicating your strategy to employees and suppliers.

The next step is to find suitable measures that can be used to measure if the company is actually obtaining its objectives. These measures are monitored at a specific frequency, i.e. once a month or quarterly.

**The Balanced Scorecard-in detail**

The BSC originators, Kaplan and Norton, describe the innovation of the balanced scorecard as follows:

*"The balanced scorecard retains traditional financial measures. But financial measures tell the story of past events. These financial measures are inadequate, however, for guiding and evaluating the journey that modern organisations must make to create future value through investment in customers, suppliers, employees, processes, technology and innovation."*

As seen below, there are four interlocked perspectives:

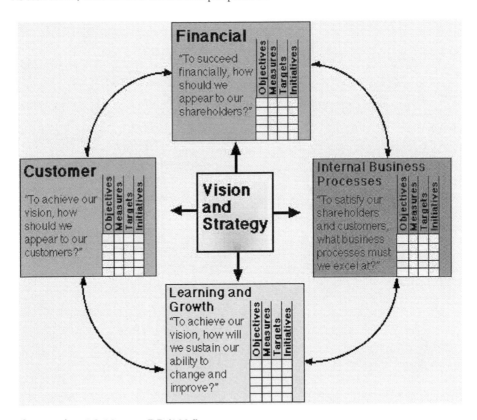

**After:** Kaplan, RS, Norton, DP (1996)

Looking at each of these four perspectives further, then:

1) **The learning and growth perspective** includes employee training and corporate cultural attitudes related to both individual and corporate self-improvement. In a knowledge worker organisation, people, the only repository of knowledge, are the main resource. SRM for example, requires skilled procurement staff with excellent interpersonal skills

2) **The business process perspective** refers to internal business processes. Metrics based on this perspective allow the managers to know how well their business is running and whether its products and services conform to customer requirements.

3) **The customer perspective**, recent management philosophy has shown an increasing realisation of the importance of customer focus and customer satisfaction. It is obvious that if customers are not satisfied, they will eventually find other suppliers that will meet their needs. Poor performance from this perspective is thus a leading indicator of future decline if no corrective action is taken.

4) **The financial perspective**, Kaplan and Norton do not disregard the traditional need for financial data. Timely and accurate funding data will always be a priority and managers will do whatever necessary to provide accurate and meaningful information from it. There is perhaps a need to include additional financial related data, such as risk assessment and cost benefit data, in this category.

### The balanced scorecard and measurement

The balanced scorecard methodology builds on some key concepts of previous management ideas such as Total Quality Management (TQM), including customer defined quality, continuous improvement, employee empowerment, and primarily, measurement based management and feedback.

Deming emphasised that all business processes should be part of a system with feedback loops. The feedback data should be examined by managers to determine the causes of variation, what the processes with significant problems are, and then they can focus attention on fixing that subset of processes.

The balanced scorecard incorporates feedback around internal business process outputs, as in TQM, but also allows for feedback loops to suppliers concerning the outcomes of business strategies.

Supplier relationship management facilitates the flow of information feedback to the suppliers so that corrective action can take place for continuous improvement.

Overleaf is an example of a supplier-rating scorecard from Phillips:

# SUPPLIER TOTAL QUALITY PERFORMANCE MEASUREMENT

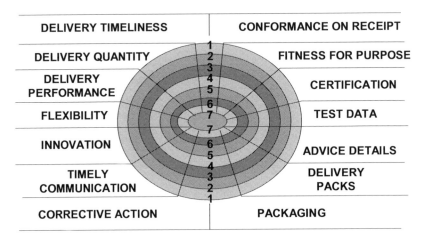

| DELIVERY TIMELINESS | CONFORMANCE ON RECEIPT |
| DELIVERY QUANTITY | FITNESS FOR PURPOSE |
| DELIVERY PERFORMANCE | CERTIFICATION |
| FLEXIBILITY | TEST DATA |
| INNOVATION | ADVICE DETAILS |
| TIMELY COMMUNICATION | DELIVERY PACKS |
| CORRECTIVE ACTION | PACKAGING |

**PHILLIPS**

As is well known, you cannot improve what you cannot measure. So metrics must be developed based on the priorities of the strategic plan and supply chain metrics in particular, for managing suppliers to allow for effective SRM. Processes are then designed to collect information relevant to these Supply Chain key performance indicators (KPIs).

## Procurement KPIs

In an approximate order of priority, these are as follows:

- Negotiated cost reduction savings
- Implemented cost reduction savings
- Cost avoidance
- Procurement ROI (savings/operating costs)
- Percentage of suppliers accounting for 80% of spending
- Supplier performance (price, delivery, quality, service)
- Contract compliance
- Requisition, PO, or invoice transaction volume
- Subjective feedback (structured, survey based)

The important thing is to select a few appropriate measures from each category and then to look at them as a set, not individually. Also, try to measure by process rather than by function. Using the 5 rights can assist on this.

### The 5 rights and key performance indicators
Key performance indicators (KPIs) can be used to ensure control of all procurement activity and highlight any deviation from the standards expected. The actual KPIs used will depend

on the product or service being purchased and they can then be monitored to ensure supplier interest is maintained in the contract and also to build historical data for reference.

In general terms, the KPIs will cover those five rights of quality, quantity, price, place and time aspects, related to the goods being purchased; examples follow:

**Quality** includes:
- Re-work
- Rejects
- Warranties
- Procedures
- Complaints
- Control

**Quantity** includes:
- Full or Part order receipts
- Discounts
- Minimum order levels

**Price** includes:
- Consumables
- Tooling
- Overtime
- Re-work
- Materials
- Labour
- Downtime
- Absenteeism

**Place** includes:
- Accuracy of delivery to location
- Tracking availability whilst in transit

**Time** includes:
- Lead-times
- Emergency response
- Set-up

## Case Study: BP KPI Scorecard

Below is an example of a KPI scorecard for Drilling Services.

| Key Areas | Section Weight % | KPI weight in section | Key Performance Indicator (KPI) | Target | Actual Score | Score % Within Section | Total Score |
|---|---|---|---|---|---|---|---|
| HSE | 40 | 15 | Safety Observations | 100 | 90 | 13.50 | 94.00 |
| | | 15 | % of offshore employees trained | 95 | 90 | 14.20 | 94.00 |
| | | 20 | Recordable Accidents per month | 0 | 0 | 20.00 | 94.00 |
| | | 15 | Non-recordable Accidents per month | 0 | 1 | 11.30 | 94.00 |
| | | 25 | Lost Time Incidents per month | 0 | 0 | 25.00 | 94.00 |
| | | 10 | Environmental Incidents per month | 0 | 0 | 10.00 | 94.00 |
| Cost | 10 | 50 | Actual v planned (% Difference) | 0% | 0% | 50.00 | 90.00 |
| | | 50 | Actual planned (% Difference) | 0% | 12% | 40.00 | 90.00 |
| Efficiency | 25 | 50 | Average % Rig NPT per month | 5 | 3 | 50.00 | 100.00 |
| | | 50 | Actual versus planned job time (%) | 10 | 9 | 50.00 | 100.00 |
| Quality | 25 | 20 | Incorrect equipment occurrences | 0 | 0 | 20.00 | 100.00 |
| | | 20 | late equipment/In excess of 3 days | 0 | 0 | 20.00 | 100.00 |
| | | 15 | Test unsuccessfully 1st attempt | 0 | 0 | 15.00 | 100.00 |
| | | 20 | # of failed removals/landings | 0 | 0 | 20.00 | 100.00 |
| | | 10 | # of failed landings on 1st attempt | 0 | 0 | 10.00 | 100.00 |
| | | 15 | # of failed tree test on 1st attempt | 0 | 0 | 15.00 | 100.00 |

Score    96.58

**BP Egypt (2008)**

These KPIs are measurable and therefore are objective criteria. They highlight area for further improvement. Subjective criteria may also be involved based on the buyer's perception, for example to commitment, attitudes and mannerisms including:

- Motivation toward individual contract commitments, future business etc.
- Response to constructive criticism, problem solving.
- Input into problem solving, innovation.

Recent studies have shown that if buyers communicate as openly as possible with their suppliers about what they expect, they will be given more information on such areas as stock levels, lead-times and quality problems.

Additionally surveys can be used to collate subjective opinions; for example the supplier survey mentioned below. Here the entire supply chain performance can be measured and the following Supply Chain KPIs can be used:

## Supply Chain key performance indicators

| Description | Measurement tool | Definition | Units |
|---|---|---|---|
| Customer orders fulfilment | On time/in Full rate (OTIF) | % orders OTIF | % |
| | Lead-time | Receipt of order to despatched/delivered | Hours/Days |
| Customer satisfaction | Customer Survey | A sampling survey to ask for customers experiences, for example: -Support available -Product availability -Flexibility -Reliability -Consistency -Comparison to the competition | % satisfied |
| Supply management | On time/in full (OTIF). | As above | % |
| | Supplier Survey. | A sampling survey to ask for suppliers experiences, for example: as in the above customer survey | % satisfied |
| | Effectiveness. | Year over year improvements | % |
| | Lead-time | Time placed order- time available for use | Hours/Days |
| Inventory (measure for each holding place of raw materials, work in progress and finished goods) | Forecast accuracy. | Actual/Forecast sales per SKU. | % |
| | Availability. | Ordered / Delivered Per SKU. | % |
| | On hand. | Value on hand/daily delivered value. | Days |
| Cash flow | Cash to cash. | Time from paying suppliers, to time paid by customers | Days |
| Quality | Quality. | Non conformances, as appropriate | Per 100 or 1000 or million |
| Operations | Utilisations. | Used/Available. | } Units } Hours } Costs |
| | Productivity. | Actual/Standard. | |
| | Costs. | Actual/Standard. | |
| | Lead-times. | Time start/time completed per operation. | Hours or Days |
| People Relationships | Internal. | Absence rates | % |
| | External. | Sampling Survey, as customers / suppliers above. | % satisfied |
| Costs | Total supply chain or per operation cost. | Cost per time period/ Units. | £ per unit |

## KPIs reporting structures

The reporting structure should ensure that, deviations from the KPIs are clearly and easily communicated both in a cost efficient manner and as acceptable time frame. The reporting structure should link the supplier, buyer and customer in a horizontal visible frame. Meanwhile, the operational, tactical and strategic levels should be linked in the vertical hierarchy.

Software can meet this need whilst a simple visual system can give adequate information in an appropriate format. For example, the 'Traffic High Light System' uses colour codes to report performance:

Green = Acceptable
Amber = Cautionary
Red = Unacceptable

This simple system can be implemented quickly and easily as a basis for more comprehensive performance measurement:

## Supplier "A"

|               | Jan   | Feb   | March | April | May   | June  |
| ------------- | ----- | ----- | ----- | ----- | ----- | ----- |
| Quality       | Green | Green | Amber | Green | Green | Green |
| Delivery      | Red   | Amber | Red   | Green | Green | Green |
| Quantity      | Green | Green | Green | Green | Amber | Green |
| Price         | Green | Amber | Green | Green | Green | Green |
| Communication | Green | Amber | Red   | Green | Amber | Green |

## KPIs and Suppliers

Once key performance indicators (KPIs) have been established and a system created, the relevant parties will need to adhere to the process. If a significant change is involved, this should include a timed plan for the introduction and induction of individuals with identified responsibilities within the process. Responsibility levels, lines of communication and reporting should also be included.

The supplier will need to commit to the programme and to recognise its advantages; for example, the performance measurements should also be of benefit to them.

The customer and any other interested parties must provide the required information expediently and recognise the benefits they will gain in terms of improved performance, reduced costs and greater co-operation. Without the co-operation of the customer and the other links in the supply chain, it can be impossible to collect the necessary data.

Supplier rating schemes, also rely on the participation of the supplier and the buyer's internal activities, (which both include goods in and despatch), along with the customer. Opposite is an example of a supplier rating scorecard:

# SUN MICROSOFT – SUPPLIER PERFORMANCE

| QUALITY PERFORMANCE (30) | ACTUAL | MAX PTS |
|---|---|---|
| TOTAL FAILURE RATE (DPM) | | 25.0 |
| FAILURE ANALYSIS | | 5.0 |
| FIELD ISSUE/PURGE/STOP SHIP | | (15.0) |
| DELIVERY PERFORMANCE (30) | | |
| LEAD TIME | | 10.0 |
| ON TIME DELIVERY | | 15.0 |
| FLEXIBILITY | | 5.0 |
| TECHNOLOGY PERFORMANCE (25) | | |
| CAPABILITIES | | 6.0 |
| CORRECTIVE ACTION/FAILURE ANALYSIS | | 10.0 |
| CONTINUOUS IMPROVEMENT | | 9.0 |
| SUPPORT PERFORMANCE (15) | | |
| PURCHASING/MATERIALS SUPPORT | | 10.00 |
| SUSTAINING TECHNICAL SUPPORT | | 5.0 |
| PERFORMANCE MATRIX TOTAL | | 100 |

**Sun Microsoft**

## KPIs: Effects on Suppliers

Suppliers must be given a thorough introduction to the supplier rating programme and understand their role. They must be encouraged to ask questions and be given thorough answers, so that, they can implement the process with little or no delays/errors. The buyer in turn will need to understand the supplier's strategies and objectives in order to apply the performance measurements and improvements effectively; of course, this information may have already been learnt when sourcing the supplier.

The supplier must be able to trust the buyer where the cost of commitment is substantial. For small to medium enterprises, the amount of effort and resources required for monitoring and maintaining performance measurement might be overwhelming; buyers should take this into account.

## KPIs: Effects on Customers

Customers/users must also understand the value of performance measurement and recognise their role. Customers and other activities must interact with procurement as part of the responsibilities of an internally integrative supply chain.

Customers will need to be shown the benefits and cost savings and added value should be demonstrated. Equally the customer should be made aware that poor supplier performance that is not reported; would result in continued poor service.

The buyer can prioritise the customer's needs in order to maximise the benefits for them. Therefore in addition to understanding the suppliers' viewpoint, they will have to understand the customer.

**Monitoring Supplier Performance**

Supplier performance should be measured over a period that is sufficient to capture any trends or fluctuations, such as seasonality. This however may not be necessary for projects to be completed within a specific time frame.

Performance monitoring must be a set objective, for which individual buyers must take responsibility. Each buyer can be given the responsibility of monitoring individual agreements or suppliers. Alternatively, the responsibility for monitoring, as an activity, may be given to an individual or specialist team.

Information must be gathered, stored and distributed in an acceptable format. It should be available to management and suppliers on a regular basis. Quantitative information on time and costs must be distributed to both suppliers and customers. This information should also take into account the quality expected from the supplier in terms of commitment and attitude. Measurement should be made against historical data and projected improvements. The supplier should be driven toward continuous improvement to remain competitive; they should not be driven towards bankruptcy by making increasing and unrealistic demands.

Comparisons can be made against similar suppliers to create a league table of performance, this information being controlled for confidentiality reasons.

**Downgrading Supplier Ratings**

Suppliers, who fail to keep within the set tolerances, must be notified within an agreed timescale. They should be given details of the non-compliance including dates and times. The supplier must also be informed of their reviewed grade and the records updated. This can be used to trigger a closer analysis of the supplier's performance to ensure the situation does not deteriorate.

The supplier needs to be given the opportunity to explain why they have failed to perform and where the deviation is severe, a meeting should be arranged to resolve the problem. The buyer should give the supplier guidance on how to achieve the required standard; this could include advice, co-operation, and the sharing of knowledge.

Where the supplier has to improve then a time scale should be set; additionally regular meetings may be necessary until the problem has been corrected, and the supplier can assure adherence to the expected performance requirements. Contingency plans may need to be drawn up in case of any recurrence.

**Upgrading Supplier Ratings**

Suppliers who have maintained or improved their performance should always be informed and thanked, for example:

'A' class suppliers should be commended.
'B' class suppliers should be upgraded.
'C' class suppliers should be upgraded.

Good suppliers can be encouraged to sustain their efforts and similar suppliers gauged against the improvements attained by others. This information can be discussed with these improved suppliers to try to identify improvement opportunities. This important concept of supplier development is considered in greater detail in part 4.0 of this book.

Increased performance should be rewarded and rewards used as an incentive for suppliers to maintain and exceed the performance expected. Acknowledging suppliers' efforts is important in building relationships. The rewards may be intrinsic in value such as, a certificate of achievement or other publicity. Buying organisations can create promotional contests to highlight the importance of performance improvement.

Substantial improvements or innovations may justify longer contracts, or other business opportunities. The buyer should always be looking for suppliers who can compete in tomorrow's market place. This will assist the buyer's organisation in staying ahead of the competition.

Longer term contracts and repeat business reflects the aims of modern procurement practice such as, reducing the supplier base for critical items and forge closer working relationships where both the supplier and buyer are committed to continuous improvement.

**Reviewing Supplier Performance**
Supplier performance measurement methods should be regularly reviewed, to ensure that it is still in line with organisational strategy and company policy. Review meetings should be agreed with suppliers and customers/users and form part of the contract. For critical items regular reviews will be necessary. The performance information collated will create a "performance profile" which will be invaluable to the buyer when analysing potential and existing buyers and for determining standards.

The suppliers' opinion of their own performance, as well as that of the buyers' organisation, should be taken into account. Where suppliers are undertaking identical measurement themselves, then the comparisons should present no surprises, thus removing any conflicts of the "you did/I did not" nature. This can assist the buyer in making improvements to their internal supply chain, so also demonstrating a good working relationship with suppliers and assisting in the promotion of their organisation to other suppliers, as a quality client.

Supplier performance needs to be monitored in a positive manner to motivate better results; indeed any preferred long-term relationships will only succeed where both parties are committed to continuous improvement.

The determination therefore of the performance required from suppliers and the related supply chain activity is important for the whole business and must therefore be something that is agreed with all parties and departments involved. This of course also includes agreement with suppliers and internal users /customers.

Objective measurement will then enable accurate reporting and correction of deviations from expected standards. They will remove subjective opinion and any "you did, I did not" game plays and works towards achieving joint agreements on any variations with subsequent joint improvements.

# The Relationship Positioning Tool

As mentioned earlier, in order to improve the supply chain more effectively, we must have a two-way measurement, which is an honest appraisal of each partner's performance in a no-blame culture. A very useful tool for this purpose is the Relationship Positioning Tool (RPT) (**Source: Douglas and Macbeth 1993**).

Organisations can only increase their own competitiveness and performance by continuously improving the performance of the other members of their supply chains. Whilst the focus of competitiveness has understandably been more traditionally directed downstream towards customers, many have failed and still fail to recognise the considerable advantages to be gained from a closer involvement with suppliers.

The aim should be to have all of the organisations in a supply chain performing to the highest levels, for example, 100 percent quality and delivery and at a reducing overall cost. Such a chain would also operate with minimum lead-time and give maximum response to meet the customer demand.

The Relationship Positioning Tool is a technique which measures the relationship between an organisation and its suppliers. It identifies the strengths and weaknesses in the customer supplier relationship and encourages discussion between customer and supplier personnel in a way that avoids making "it personal" and blaming individuals.

RPT enables the customer and supplier organisations to create a joint agenda for improvement activities, including supplier development and buying organisation development. Whilst a 100% management effectiveness of parties that are not owned, can never be absolute or be dictated, it can be e gained through a willingness to collaborate. Attitudes of collaboration, sharing and open communication will then need to replace traditional adversarial practices, which tend to assume that product, services, suppliers and employees, are interchangeable and are therefore easily discarded when times are difficult.

Managers can have difficulties in understanding the full range of issues inherent in managing their supply chains. Additionally they can have difficulty in knowing where to start to make those needed changes that will increase the effectiveness of their supply chains. RPT addresses both these difficulties, by analysing the current situation between a company and a supplier and pinpoints aspects of the relationship that needs to be improved.

Where there are adverse variations from pre determined targets for quality, delivery and cost of supplied goods, then this represents waste and weaknesses in the relationship between suppliers and customers. Similarly, the relationship has to be effective in a way, which ensures continuous improvement, through innovation, is undertaken.

The potential of the relationship to continuously improve to achieve present and future demands with respect to quality, delivery, cost and innovation is dependent upon the following:

- The strategy developed by the customer. This can be measured in terms of the attitude adopted towards the supplier, how the customer's requirements are specified and how these are supported through systems and people.
- The capability of the supplier to provide goods/services at the right quality, the right time and at the lowest overall cost. This is measured in terms of the overall company profile, people skills and organisation, process capability and supplier management

The customer's and suppliers ability to create a flow of information to the supplier provides the basis for the effective transfer of goods/services and for the sharing of knowledge and ideas. Aspects of these information flows are technical, involvement with the supplier, business and the people who make the contacts

The major contributory factors are made up of major roots, such as company profile, people, process, and supplier management, and the elements of the RPT "Tree" model divide into minor roots. For example, under the supplier capability, the following processes are examined.

- Design
- Plant capability
- Plant capacity
- Systems
- Process range
- Flexibility
- Lead-times

### Generating and using the RPT scores

As with any analysis procedure, data has to be gathered to provide a base of information on which the identification of strengths and weaknesses can take place. Two questionnaires, one for the customer and one for the supplier, gather over 300 pieces of data. Each response to a question is then scored against "best practice" by a third party. From these collected scores, the strengths and weaknesses of the relationship can be identified and areas for improvement identified for both sides.

By opening up the possibility of a free and open interchange of views on the results; to which both have contributed, the exercise rapidly develops into a mutual self help process in which both sides see value, since they have already recognised that each must change to some degree to effect the best possible improvements.

## Review and Control of long-term contracts

One of the most challenging tasks for procurement is the management of long term service contracts, including outsourcing agreements. These types of contracts can last for up to five or 10 years, during which time the business needs and risks may change significantly. Therefore, one of the most important controls that a purchaser can put in place is a robust contract management structure. This will provide a framework for regular communication between the parties. It should provide a mechanism for regular reviews of the service, price and strategy, with a facility to agree any necessary adjustments to meet these new challenges. It should also provide an escalation structure for managing any disputes.

To ensure the correct type and level of service delivery, it is vital that the product, the services and their relevant service levels are clearly detailed. The supplier/provider should also be required to provide regular performance reports for the buyer/purchaser. It is relatively easy to set demanding service levels, but it is also most important to monitor them regularly.

It is also essential that the contract contains a tailored mechanism that incentivises a supplier's performance. The most successful long-term service contracts contain not only disincentives against poor performance but also incentives to improve it. The following questions may therefore be asked:

- What types of performance do we require?
- Does the contract incentivise these?
- What do we want to pay?
- Does the contract reflect this and protect us against unexpected price increases?
- Does the contract easily allow us to source our services elsewhere and/or terminate the contract?
- Does the contract contain exit provisions?
- How will the relationship be managed?

### Measurement and Review Process

Both parties must put in a great deal of work to make a contract relationship work. The following diagram depicts one continuum of relationship types:

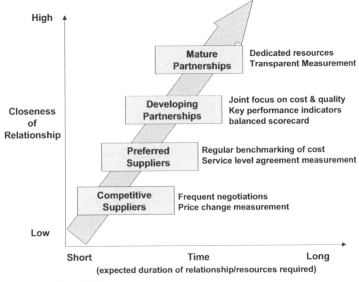

**After:** Searles (2003)

The key steps that can be applied to supplier relationships are as follows:

1) Define the target and desired results
2) The goal measurement
3) Developing the measures
4) Agree the reporting methods
5) Review the process agreement
6) Issue the report
7) Refine and review the process

Let us now look at these in turn.

*1) Define the target and desired results.* This first step is to establish clearly defined targets, as they lay the foundation for the relationship and ensure that both organisations are aware of their responsibilities. Goals should be set for the short, medium and long terms. The buyer and supplier should come to a joint decision and prevent unrealistic targets.

*2) The goal measurement.* Procurement relies on other functions for this measurement. Achieving each goal may require several initiatives running in parallel across different functions in both organisations.

*3) Developing the measures.* All those involved must agree the basic aspects of the process and what aspects of hard and soft measurement form they should take:

- Hard, objective measures will typically be quantitative, for example, percentage of deliveries received on time, delivery quality in parts per million, the value of annual cost improvements.
- Soft measures may require more subjective judgment and can be used to measure how the overall nature of the relationships is developing. Examples are management attitude, flexibility to changing business needs and a proactive approach to problem solving and resolution. One feature of many measurement and review processes that is often overlooked is the supplier's commitment and effort to making the relationship work.

To check each measure, the following questions can be asked:
- The Measure, is it clear with a clear title?
- Purpose, why is it being measured?
- Relates to: which business objective does this measure relate to?
- Target, what is to be achieved, and by when?
- Formula, what is the formula or rationale used?
- Frequency, how often should the measure be used?
- Who measures, who is responsible for collection and reporting, and who is the source?
- Who acts, who is responsible for taking action?
- What to do, what action should be taken?

*4) Agreeing the reporting methods.* Unfortunately, all too often, the contract manager is usually appointed when the contract has been placed, having had no, or at best, little pre-contract involvement. They will frequently therefore not have any real experiences of effective contract management. Consequently here, the contract management structure is inadequate and the contract manager is then at a disadvantage with their opposite number on the supplier's team in terms of experience and training. As a result there is often no agreement as to reporting methods and many of the following questions are not agreed.

- Who does what?
- For whom?
- When and where?
- At what cost and for what price?
- To what quality?
- For how long?
- Against what performance measures?
- Under what monitoring arrangements?

*5) Review the process agreement.* Within a typical strategic relationship, there will often need to be two types of review, strategic and operational.

- Strategic reviews which are usually held once or twice a year, involving senior management from both parties with a wide ranging agenda focusing on future goals and direction, but also dealing with any consistent failures.
- Operational reviews are typically held every month or quarter. The focus of the meetings here should be the performance against targets set for the year and actions to improve any areas of weakness. This will be discussed in further detail later in this section.

*6) Issue the report.* A successful review meeting should focus on looking at how previous processes and practices can be improved for the future.

*7) Refine and review the process.* An effective process has to be reviewed regularly, no less than once a year, to ensure that objectives continue to accurately reflect the business needs. Targets on continuing objectives should be increased in line with improvements in performance.

### Reviews and visits process

An accurate evaluation of a supplier's current and potential capabilities, intentions and aspirations can only really be measured by a detailed knowledge of their operations. In many organisations, buyers rarely meet sales personnel at the supplier's premises, thereby minimising their opportunities to become familiar with the supplier's capabilities.

A well-planned visit builds and strengthens an existing relationship as well as organisations the commitment of the current suppliers or the potential of any future ones. Such regular reviews are essential to facilitate continuous improvement. Post contract, they provide a platform for challenge and discussion of price, establishment of cost data, mutual discussions on value and risk sharing and sustaining continuous improvement.

The following circumstances for reviews and visits can be identified:

| Circumstance | Reason for visit |
|---|---|
| A new or potential suppler | To assess their capabilities and commitments |
| A change in location of the supplier | To ensure consistent performance |
| A change in key supplier personnel | To reconfirm the supplier's goals and commitments and/or capabilities |
| An issue with the relationship | To organise a longer term commitment with the supplier, or, to acknowledge a breach or failure to live up to the relationship understanding |
| To develop and/or deliver a performance challenge | To develop data and a cost analysis<br>To identify additional value propositions |
| A large scale supply issue | To facilitate communication and agree action |
| To initiate or maintain a development programme | To identify and agree the areas that need to be improved.<br>To provide systems support and guidance, or,<br>To measure progress against those plans |

Supplier visits will be symbolic or practical aspects, for example:

- Symbolic visits focus on the state of the relationship and usually involve senior management and key users of the goods/ services provided as well as procurement staff. Symbolic visits focus on building and strengthening the relationship, involving significant conditioning of the supplier beforehand, and a clear formal agenda. These visits are used to either to celebrate the achievements of, or discuss breaches in the relationship.

- Practical visits focus on operational issues, such as data collection, performance assessment and improvement. Practical visits are while still planned, are regarded as routine, management of the contract and relationship and focus on performance improvements, ideally involving key users, R&D, marketing and production.

Meetings will also be based on pre contract or post contract issues:

- Pre-contract issues at meetings will cover the following:

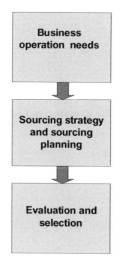

**Business operation needs**

**Sourcing strategy and sourcing planning**

**Evaluation and selection**

**Symbolic**
- Encouraging potential suppliers
- Raising supply base awareness
  - Creating competition

**Practical**
- Informing the supply base of our needs
  - Understanding the supplier's goals
    - Benchmarking
  - Constructing supplier capability profiles
Developing component analysis data

• Post-contract issues for meetings will cover the following:

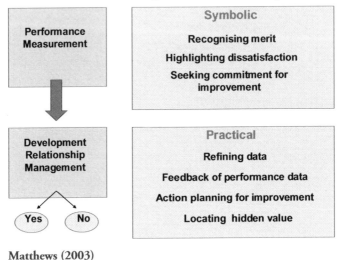

**Matthews (2003)**

Targeted and sustained improvement effort will be unlikely without the regular flow of standardised and objective performance information back to the supplier, covering the agreed key performance indicators.

A structured programme of supplier reviews and visits will provide the impetus for a whole series of practical follow up action plans aimed at the delivery of the mutually agreed targets:

## Case Study - BP Supplier Performance Management process

Category Management of Business Support Services for BP uses a Supplier Performance Management (SPM) process and upon implementation for one category of indirect support services, one business unit recorded a 30% improvement in efficiency, costs and lead-times. BP's SPM is comprised of the following stages:

1. Supplier Prioritisation
Using Kraljic, they highlight the key suppliers for immediate attention for the process.

2. Competent organisation
This ensures the procurement function for the category, have the required skills and competences for effective supplier management and full knowledge of the principles of Supplier Relationship Management.

3. Measures and Targets
Measures and Targets are clearly identified and agreed with the supplier base so that realistic KPIs can be established.

4. Performance Review Process.
Regular reviews and meetings are built into the process, so that both sides have regular feedback on performance, in order that the appropriate action plans for improvement can be implemented.

5. Drive and Sustain Value.
This recognises that monitoring of performance and continuous improvement activities should be on-going despite inevitable changes in processes and personnel, additionally, value-added needs to be managed through the SPM process.

# Benchmarking

*"Benchmarking is the process of continuously measuring and comparing one's business processes against comparable processes in leading organisations to obtain information that will help the organisation identify and implement improvements."*

The steps in the benchmarking of processes recommended by CIPS (Chartered Institute of Purchasing and Supply) are as follows:

- Determining what customers really want.
- Realistically assessing competition.
- Identifying best practice.
- Learning from other business sectors.
- Introducing relevant best practice.
- Providing a means to constant improvement.

# Case Study - Motorola

All Motorola plants exchange benchmarking information in the following areas:
- Cycle time
- Scrap
- Productivity
- Warehouse performance-in particular, cycle time and quality
- Procurement performance

Benchmarking is against Motorola business units and external benchmarking partners.

Andersen and Gaute-Pettersen (1996) summarise benchmarking into five steps that has been drawn from Deming's approach:

1) **Plan:** this is selecting a process to be benchmarked, forming a team to do the benchmarking, documenting the process to be benchmarked and establishing measures of performance for the process.

113

2) **Search:** listing the criteria to identify a benchmarking partner, identifying the partners, selecting a partner and establishing a contact.

3) **Observe:** determine information needs and where the information can be found, deciding what/how to gather and record the information, carrying out the gathering.

4) **Analyse:** this is putting the information previously gathered into a useful format and using it to identify the gaps in one's own performance.

5) **Adapt:** this involves the process of effecting an improvement in one's own processes and performance. It involves setting targets, planning and implementing change.

Benchmarking, therefore, can be seen as a continuous improvement/Kaizen style process, so that improvements, once attained, are not a reason for leaving the process. Further improvements should be sought because other suppliers are also continually improving and so that it forms a continuous cycle, as shown below in Deming's PDCA cycle:

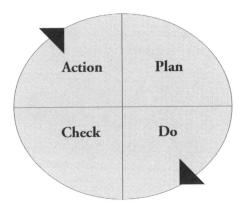

In this normal PDCA cycle, each step covers the following:

**Plan**
- Clarify objectives
- Decide the mans to achieve objectives (develop plans)

**Do**
- Execute plans

**Check**
- Check if plans were executed as expected
- Check if objectives were achieved as planned

**Action**
- If objectives were not met, analyse the results and develop counter measures
- Where objectives are met, then this develops standards of performance.

With benchmarking this PDCA cycle then becomes:

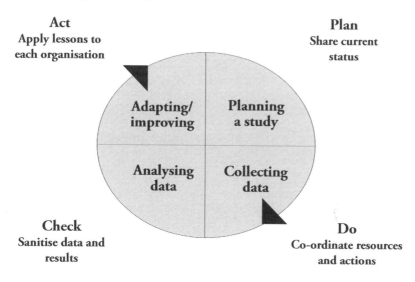

The following diagram depicts how different levels of implementation of benchmarking with suppliers, using a co-ordinated team approach, can deliver world class service levels, TQM and, a continuously improving supply chain.

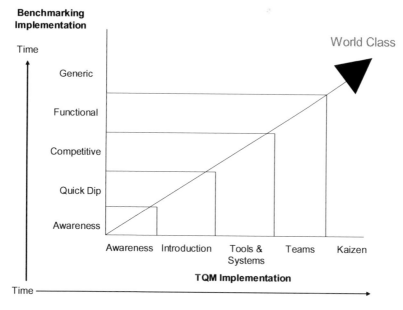

**Source:** Baumber, C.S. 1993

A classic example of this is the following case study from BA.

## Case Study: British Airways

BA continuously benchmarks against their competitors in terms of financial information and service provided.

The analysis covers a range of activities including:
- In-flight food
- Aircraft cleaning
- Fuel costs

In collaboration with their suppliers, BA works out action plans to constantly improve. BA would like to be customer of first choice for their key suppliers, and they see that the only way to become this and to maintain it, is to collaborate closely, share information, and to mutually share risk and reward.

This is continually applied as the PDCA cycles shown on previous pages.

The diagram below shows how Kaizen and benchmarking approaches can deliver improved results over time, and are therefore essential pre-requisites to be incorporated into a an SRM approach.

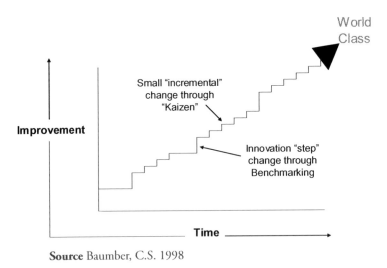

**Source** Baumber, C.S. 1998

A simple benchmarking methodology is shown as follows:

Stage 5 - Incorporate findings
CHANGE they way you do things

Stage 4 - How do they do it?
Find out what is different

Stage 3 - Who is BEST in class
Measure the competition

Stage 2 - Measure and analyse
Find out how YOU do it

Stage 1 - Plan the Investigation
Decide what to benchmark

## Types of Benchmarking
There are six types of benchmarking and these are explained below:

### 1) Internal Benchmarking Awareness/Quick dip
This arises when one part of an organisation compares its performance with other parts of the same organisation. A good example would be where one company in a group of organisations compares itself with other members of the grouping terms of their supplier performance. The obvious disadvantage to this form of benchmarking is that practice within the group might not be superior to the best existing beyond the group's boundaries.

### 2) Competitive Benchmarking
This is when competitors agree to benchmark their processes. They might agree to compare how they manage their supplier relationships and how they implement SRM. There is an obvious reluctance to do this in many cases.

### 3) Functional Benchmarking
This is when organisations compare functions, such as procurement and supply, finance, personnel, with similar functions in other, possibly dissimilar organisations. SRM benchmarking would be a good example here so that organisations can compare different approaches and gaps.

### 4) Generic Process Benchmarking
This is similar to functional benchmarking but compares individual processes rather than whole functions.

### 5) Core Competencies Benchmarking
In this case core competencies are compared and in respect of SRM, such an analysis might lead to greater outsourcing, which requires a closer working relationship with those preferred partners.

### 6) Customer Benchmarking

This compares the organisation's performance against the expectations of customers.

### Barriers to Benchmarking

These can include the following:

- Fear of disclosing competitive information. Suppliers can be reluctant to open their books and become more transparent.
- A view that the organisation is already the best. This can be as a result of a lack of performance measurement, particularly in the area of supplier performance and its effects on total costs of ownership.
- Lack of support and understanding within the organisation of benchmarking and with SRM generally.
- Difficulty in implementing the process properly because it needs a lot of time and resources. Organisations often under-estimate or do not know the benefits of benchmarking in terms of more effective SRM.
- Lack of information concerning the current situation. As mentioned elsewhere in this book, a lack of effective contract management leads to a lack of supplier performance measurement.
- Lack of relevant supply chain KPIS

Best in class organisations have formal criteria for the evaluation of existing suppliers as part of a structured SRM approach, and continually compare them to the performance of alternative suppliers.

# Part three: Summary

- Supplier Relationship Management (SRM) is the management of the whole interface between supply and buying organisations through the whole life of the contract. The aim is to achieve maximum long-term contribution from the supplier that works towards achieving the buying organisation's strategic goals.

- The Balanced Scorecard methodology builds on some key concepts of previous management ideas such as Total Quality Management (TQM), including customer defined quality, continuous improvement, employee empowerment, and primarily, measurement based management and feedback.

- Key performance indicators (KPIs) can be used to ensure control of all procurement activity and highlight any deviation from the standards expected.

- The actual KPIs used will depend on the product or service being purchased and they can then be monitored to ensure supplier interest is maintained in the contract and also to build historical data for reference

- The Relationship Positioning Tool is a technique which measures the relationship between an organisation and its suppliers. It identifies the strengths and weaknesses in the customer supplier relationship and encourages discussion between customer and supplier personnel in a way that avoids making "it personal" and blaming individuals.

- Benchmarking is the process of continuously measuring and comparing one's business processes against comparable processes in leading organisations to obtain information that will help the organisation identify and implement improvements.

# Part four: Supplier Development

As we will see, the wide range of supplier development activities involve varying degrees of procurement input and resource.

## Definitions

There are many versions of definitions for supplier development, but as you can see below, they all contain the similar means to achieve the same objective.

*"Supplier development is the process of working with certain suppliers on a one to one basis to improve their performance for the benefit of the buying organisation."*

*"Supplier development is supporting the supplier in enhancing the performance of their products and services or improving the supplier's capabilities."*

*"Supplier development is a long term cooperative effort between a buying organisation and its suppliers to upgrade the suppliers' technical, quality, delivery and cost capabilities and to foster ongoing improvements."*

Meanwhile for the purposes on this book, supplier development will be defined as:

*"Any effort of a buying organisation towards a supplier that will increase the supplier's performance and/or capabilities, to meet short and/or long-term needs of the buyer."*

## Reasons for Supplier Development

There are very good and sound reasons for embarking on a supplier development process and these are as follows:

* Improving supplier performance.
* Reducing costs.
* Resolving serious quality issues.
* Developing new routes to supply.
* Improving business alignment between the supplier and the buying organisation.
* Developing a product or service not currently available in the marketplace.
* Generating competition for a high price product or service dominating the marketplace.

Supplier development should therefore lead to improvements in the total added value from the supplier, in terms of:

* Product or services offered.
* Business processes and performance.

- Improvements in lead-times and delivery.

## Various approaches

There is no single approach to supplier development. Procurement and supply management professionals must select the most appropriate approach to suit their relationship with the supplier that they have selected for development. There are therefore different types of, and approaches to, supplier development and these are appropriate for different supply markets.

Supplier development involves embracing supplier expertise and aligning it to the buying organisation's business need, and, where appropriate, vice versa. The objectives for development can be relatively minor, such a slight adjustments in staffing levels, or very substantial such as the appraisal and re-launch of an entire range of critical products.

A supplier development project might involve developing a supplier's business such as helping the supplier to evaluate and redesign their corporate strategy. The purpose of this might be to align the supplier very closely and on a long-term basis with the buying organisation in a strategic alliance or joint venture. A case study will provide an example of this:

## Case Study: BAE Systems

A development for BAE Systems when building navy submarines is their Performance Partnering Arrangement (PPA). This has improved deals with major suppliers by providing more certainty for longer-term contracts and a gain share /pain share deal.

Pre-PPA supplier relationships were more adversarial. The problem was that suppliers were competing for contracts on the basis they would work, for instance, on one project but maybe not on the next. Inevitably this pushed up costs. It took time to convince the suppliers that BAE would use their equipment on future boat building work.

For the suppliers working under PPA, the situation changed as BAE commit to a supplier for the duration of the class of boat this is being built. As long as they hit quality, cost delivery and technical innovation targets, mutual gains are shared.

The transformation in supplier relations came about suddenly and urgently. Previously, contracts with suppliers had been completed five or six years earlier and their focus had been on delivery. After speaking to suppliers they identified three market trends:

- That some manufacturers were going out of business,
- Others were leaving the market,
- Costs were increasing.

To find out what was causing these things, they devised a questionnaire for existing suppliers.

The results were alarming and revealed BAE was not the customer of choice it believed it was. The research concluded that unless the submarines business was attractive, then:

- a significant number of critical suppliers would not have any incentive to continue production of key equipment
- a lack of continuity of work would give rise to skills retention issues and a loss of capability
- a significant number of critical suppliers were at the risk of business failure.

The answers revealed 64 percent of suppliers gave BAE cause for concern and there was a risk that the next boat would be unaffordable.

As a result of closer collaboration, boats now cost less. BAE also were able to take out 30 percent of the material prices. A change was the introduction of supplier forums, where the top 10 suppliers cover 70 percent of spend.
These forums are held every eight weeks and enable regular communications with suppliers. The consensus among the buying team is that these meetings are successful because they instil trust.

Whatever the form of supplier development, the process may be a highly resource intensive exercise and involve for example, a steering group and various action teams, each with action plans for allocated projects and formal reporting procedures against time scales. Both organisations must share a mutual understanding, appreciation and desire to achieve the objectives of the supplier development project.

Such a project would involve the principles of change management (this topic is covered later in part 5.0 of this book) and require visible commitment from both parties' top management teams with identifiable sponsors and champions of change. It is critical to involve people with vision, imagination and commitment; to keep these involved and to ensure the project is not damaged by a change in personnel. It is also important to ensure that there is a smooth decision making process and that, where appropriate, those involved in the supplier development project from both organisations are empowered to make decisions.

Another approach to supplier development is "Reverse Marketing". One example of which is where a buying organisation encourages a supplier(s) to enter a new market. This might, for instance, involve the supplier developing its operation or introducing a new range of products.

## Selection of suppliers

The selection of suppliers for development should be dependent on:

- Category Management strategy.
- Scale of value/improvement opportunity.
- Cost, complexity and duration of value attainment.
- Supplier co-operation.

Supplier development is normally undertaken with existing suppliers that can be, and agree to being improved. The supplier's performance against agreed criteria must be measured in order to identify the scope for development at the outset and, once the development process has started, to monitor and manage improvements.

As supplier development can be a resource intensive process, it should be undertaken only with selected suppliers. It should only be undertaken with those suppliers from which real business benefit can be derived. Therefore supplier development can be a one-off project as well as on going activity that may take some years to come to fruition. Additionally, supplier development is a two-way process and should be thought of as a joint buyer/supplier development activity.

Incentives need to be given to suppliers to encourage their commitment to supplier development, such as, a reward of shared benefits, or "preferred supplier" status. In many cases, the development of the supplier will be of benefit to the supplier's other customers, some of which may be the buying organisation's competition. This in itself may be an incentive for the supplier to participate in a supplier development project, i.e. they can improve relationships with all their customers as a consequence.

**Activities**

As we have mentioned earlier, the main purpose of close, long-term relationships with suppliers is the achievement of high quality products and services that satisfy customer needs. Often, suppliers lack the abilities and competencies required to deal with the different or special standards that are now required by their buyers, therefore, supplier development is necessary. This may vary widely and can include:

- Raising performance expectations.
- Education and training on quality requirements and know-how for supplier personnel.
- Recognition of supplier's achievements and performance in the form of rewards.
- Placement of engineering and other buyer personnel at the supplier's premises.
- Direct capital investment by the buying organisation in the supplier.

We shall explore this range of activities in the following sections.

# Supplier Development Categories

The following diagram (overleaf) summarises some key categories of supplier development:

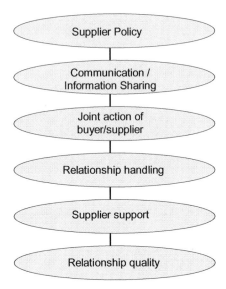

Questions can be posed in each of the above categories to form a useful survey/audit of existing supplier development activities, as follows:

### Supplier Policy

- Buy – make decision
- Establishment of long term relationships (over 5 years) with suppliers
- Supply base reduction during the last 10 years
- Supplier's performance formal evaluation
- Benchmarking of other suppliers

### Information sharing/Communication

- Frequent and informal exchange of information
- Communication includes many inter organisation contacts
- Electronic data change
- Supplier's knowledge of his products specifications
- Supplier's knowledge of his product use in buyer's final product
- Timely feedback of supplier's mistakes
- Feedback of supplier's evaluation
- Timely planning and communication of purchase programme
- Supplier certification programme

### Joint action of supplier/buyer

- Joint quality planning (e.g. product specifications, quality requirements)
- Joint production planning (e.g. JIT system)
- Supplier involvement in product development process
- Joint workgroups
- Held meetings on a regular basis to solve problems
- Conflict resolution techniques

| Relationship handling issues |
| --- |

- Systematic contact with supplier to know what is going on
- Use of formal contract
- Clear delegation of responsibilities
- Feedback from supplier regarding complaints and suggestions
- Acceptance and implementation of supplier improvement suggestions

| Supplier support |
| --- |

- Placement of buyer personnel and facilities at supplier's premises
- Advice and suggestions to supplier according to quality results
- Recognition of supplier's performance in the form of rewards
- Training/education of supplier in quality requirements, know-how

| Relationship quality |
| --- |

- The relationship is considered as a partnership
- Priority is given to quality
- Mutual trust between buyer and supplier
- Mutual awareness of other party's needs
- Goal congruence between supplier and buyer

# Partner approach

As a company's needs, supplier goals and objectives change constantly, it is unlikely that the capabilities of a supply base and the requirements of a client organisation will naturally align for any prolonged period of time. Supplier development aims to create and sustain alignment between an organisation and a supplier for the benefit of both parties.

However, effort should be focused on those key categories of spend that are most likely to deliver significant additional value to the business, as developing current or potential suppliers can be resource intensive. Using portfolio analysis to segment spend, it is relatively straightforward to determine the most appropriate categories and therefore, which suppliers to engage in a supplier development programme.

At this stage, two further factors should also be considered:

- The expected benefits from supplier development for the buyer and the supplier's ability to develop and change.
- The cost of development for both the buyer and the supplier to ensure that there is an acceptable return on investment for both of them.

Buyers will need to protect themselves from any supplier power on bottleneck items, and long term relationships built up through supplier development programmes may be a way of achieving this. This is because the expenditure is large enough to encourage supplier participation and the category's supply market is difficult to buy in, so the relationship tends to be seen as long rather than short term.

Generally, supplier development is used where there are tangible value benefits to be gained over using other suppliers in the long term, potential supply vulnerability or where suppliers are believed to have the power.

The objectives of any programme will be based largely upon the gap identified between existing supplier performance and the standard required now and in the future. The style of development can be coach, mentor or challenger, depending on the balance of expertise that exists between the buyer and the supplier.

## Progression in relationships

When there is a clear commitment to supplier development, this means it is likely the relationship between buyer and supplier will then make progress up a relationship spectrum; for example, from being competitive leverage or preferred supplier, to becoming a performance partner or even strategic alliance partner. This relationship progression being illustrated below:

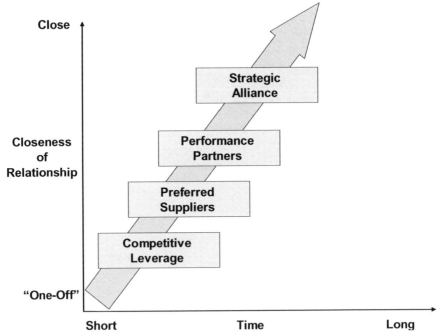

However, this progression should not occur by default. A well-structured supplier development programme should link the achievement of specific performance deliverables to discrete "steps" in this relationship progression, where suppliers receive benefits for delivering on their commitment to change and develop.

A structured approach, which could help to achieve such a progression, could contain the following drivers:

## Checklist: Creating success in relationship progression

1) Define and develop a strategy to meet the business and end customer needs.
2) Secure agreement between both parties on how the supplier can help achieve these needs.
3) Establish clear measures to gauge the supplier performance.
4) Ensure regular, detailed and action focused feedback to the supplier.
5) Agree on the supplier's current performance gap and expected performance requirements.
6) Obtain acceptance and commitment from the supplier's senior management.
7) Develop and agree a time plan with the supplier to close the performance gap.
8) Get commitment on the part of the buyer to transfer knowledge and potentially best practice to the supplier.
9) Get commitment to invest significant procurement resource in the programme.
10) Establish a multifunctional customer team that will:
    a) adhere to a common sourcing strategy and
    b) share knowledge.

Some suppliers may retain fundamental objections to the more open methods of the relationship philosophy and prefer not to change their ways, or be unable to. Meanwhile a number of different offerings can add value to the relationships, and could help to compensate for any price increases or offset them. Examples here include the following:

- Joint focus on identifying and solving the shared problem together.
- Incentivised performance and shared risk and reward.
- Product innovation, assistance with research and development, or even out sourcing responsibility for development.
- Scheduling delivery in order to support product availability.
- Consignment stock or simplified ordering and invoice processes.
- Packaging waste reclamation, reduction or both.
- Improvements and developments in product yield.
- Higher quality levels.

There are many ways to increase the value that suppliers can deliver. These will now be explained in the following sections.

## Supplier Development Practices

Buying organisations faced with problems of deficient supplier performance, can implement a wide range of supplier development practices such as, supplier evaluation and feedback, supplier recognition and supplier training. These will work towards upgrading the performance and/or capabilities of the weakest links in the supply chain.

Such activities require different levels of involvement by the buying organisation and are characterised by different levels of implementation complexity. Therefore, it could be useful to characterise supplier development activities according to their level of involvement and implementation complexity (i.e. skill, time and resources required to execute successfully a particular activity).

As supplier development broadly involves any effort by a buying organisation to improve a supplier's performance to meet the buying organisation's short and/or long term supply needs, then buyers can make use of a wide range of supplier development practices to improve a supplier's performance and/or capabilities, as shown in the following checklist:

## Checklist: Supplier development practices

- The predominance of quality over cost in selecting suppliers
- Buying from a limited number of suppliers per purchased item
- Sourcing from a few dependable suppliers,
- Providing education and/or technical assistance to suppliers,
- Long term contracts with suppliers
- Clarity of specifications provided by the buyer Supplier performance evaluation and feedback
- Parts standardisation
- Supplier certification
- Supplier reward and recognition
- Plant visits to suppliers
- Training to suppliers
- Intensive information exchange with suppliers (i.e. sharing of accounting and financial data by the supplier and sharing of internal information such as costs, quality levels, by the supplier)
- Collaborating with suppliers in materials improvement and development of new materials
- Involvement of suppliers in the buyer's new product development process

There are three other supplier development practices to be considered: direct involvement, incentives and enforced competition.

Direct involvement includes such practices as formal evaluation of the suppliers, supplier certification, site visits, supplier recognition, feedback to suppliers, training, information evaluation of suppliers, inviting supplier's personnel to the organisation's facilities, and verbal or written requests to improve performance.

The incentives factor includes the promise of current and future benefits to the supplier if performance was improved and enforced competition includes using two or three suppliers per purchased item

Since the availability of resources is always a constraint for organisations, there are different levels of supplier development practices, characterised by their degree of company involvement and amount of resources required.

# Supplier development phases

The supplier development practices shown in the above Checklist can be grouped further into three sets of practices according to the level of organisation involvement and implementation complexity (i.e. skill, time and resources required to executive successfully a particular activity). These three sets are shown in the following checklist:

## Checklist: Reactive, Proactive and Strategic Supplier Development Phases

### Reactive Supplier Development
- Reporting of supplier evaluation results to suppliers
- Sourcing from a limited number of suppliers
- Parts standardisation
- Supplier qualification process

### Proactive Supplier Development
- Plant visits to suppliers
- Supplier reward and recognition
- Collaboration with suppliers in materials improvement
- Supplier certification (ISO 9000)

### Strategic Supplier Development
- Training to suppliers
- Supplier involvement in the buyer's product design process
- Sharing of cost and quality information by the supplier
- Sharing of accounting information by the supplier
- Supplier Co-ordination

We will now look closer at the reactive, proactive and strategic development phases:

# The Reactive Supplier Development phase

The Reactive Supplier Development phase relates to those supplier development practices that require the most limited organisation involvement and minimum investment of the company's resources (i.e. personnel, time and capital) and thus, are likely to be implemented first in an effort to improve supplier performance and/or capabilities.

These supplier development practices include evaluating supplier performance, providing feedback about the results of its evaluation and sourcing from a limited number of suppliers. Parts standardisation complements sourcing from a limited number of suppliers, by increasing the volume orders with specific suppliers. Supplier qualification is generally considered to be a more informal and less stringent programme than supplier certification; consequently, it was included as a basic supplier development practice. Therefore, the Reactive Supplier Development phase included measures of evaluating supplier performance and providing feedback to suppliers, sourcing from a limited number of suppliers per purchased item, parts standardisation, and supplier qualification.

Although improvements can be made, it has been found that superior levels of service and response can be achieved by investing more time and effort in the following phases.

**Supplier Rationalisation: A process of elimination**

Supplier rationalisation is the process that organisations use to identify the optimum number of suppliers needed to fulfil their business goals. The result can either be an increase or decrease in the number of supplier used, depending on the nature of existing supplier relationships and market conditions in which they operate.

The first stage of the rationalisation process is a detailed analysis of how much is spent which each supplier.

Organisations can bundle goods together to create an attractive package of potential bidders. In addition, introducing online catalogues, where end-users ensure business compliance with the supplier, reduces the risk of maverick buying, which leads to fewer suppliers on the database.

But when using supplier rationalisation, organisations should take the following three factors into consideration:

- Contractual obligation
- Location
- Specification

First, many organisations are not fully aware of their contractual obligations and may not know that they are locked into contracts and unable to delete suppliers from their lists.

Second, in terms of location, many suppliers maintain they can offer countrywide service and support, even though the reality can be quite different. Where speed of response is a crucial business requirement, the premature elimination of a supplier before another can be validated may prove a costly mistake. Therefore an investigation of the supply market is essential.

Lastly, the specification of a product or service is a key facet of what determines high or low market difficulty on the portfolio matrix. The onus should therefore be on the owner of the specification to create a brief that can be fulfilled by a number of suppliers to create competition. The impact of specifications written in favour of one solution or supplier will reduce the opportunities to change them easily.

**Rationalisation Process**

Roberts, G (2003)

## Case Study: Laing O'Rourke cuts supply base

Construction organisation Laing O'Rourke is to cut its suppliers from 2,000 to less than 500.

It hopes the move will improve relations with a smaller group of suppliers so it can drive competitiveness and improve standards of service. It also wants to target environmental issues in its supply base and reduce waste.

The organisation will give suppliers the opportunity to get involved with projects at an early stage. It hopes they will influence design and the choice of materials and demonstrate their capabilities directly to the company's clients.

The construction industry is starting to realise the benefits of tighter management of the supply base, but explained selection is important. "We need to be consistent. We need to ensure the suppliers we select are the best fit for our ongoing business requirements. Though this we will have a greater opportunity to manage the supply base to ensure we have competitive supply conditions, greater certainty of project timing and excellent health and safety."

## Supplier base reduction: Research

More than three quarters of buyers are looking to use fewer suppliers, according to a *Supplier Management* poll. In a survey of 100 buyers, 77 percent said they were looking to make cuts to their vendor list.

Buyers considering reductions said consolidation would make the supply base more manageable and cost effective.

Supplier reduction is a legitimate activity enabling aggregation and optimisation, leading to cost reduction.

The benefits of having fewer suppliers are:

- Less administration time
- Less logistics time
- Less carbon footprint
- Less reactive buying
- Becoming a bigger fish in a few suppliers' ponds rather than a small fish in a large organisation's ocean.

To rationalise, procurement must have a good understanding of what each of their suppliers provide. The challenge in supplier rationalisation is not so much in reducing the suppliers, but in developing the category management strategy so that you are clear on what kind of suppliers you want to be left with.

# The Proactive Supplier Development phase

The Proactive Supplier Development phase refers to supplier development practices characterised by increased yet still moderate levels of buyer involvement and implementation complexity, therefore requiring comparatively more company resources (personnel, time and capital) than the Reactive Supplier Development phase.

The supplier development activities considered in this phase have moderate levels of involvement and implementation complexity including visiting suppliers' plants to assess their processes, reward and recognition of supplier's achievements in quality improvement and supplier certification.

We refer to Supplier Certification (see below for further amplification) as suppliers having ISO 9000 registration, a practice accepted by some organisations. The collaboration with suppliers in the improvement and development of new materials and components is another practice involved in this phase.

This practice contrasts with the involvement of the supplier in the buyer's new product design process which requires a higher level of involvement and implementation complexity and therefore is considered in the Strategic Supplier Development phase below. Hence, the Proactive Supplier Development phase include measures of visiting suppliers to assess their facilities, rewarding and recognising supplier's performance improvements, collaborating with suppliers in materials improvement and certification of suppliers through ISO 9000.

### Supplier Certification

Supplier Certification is a comprehensive process designed to ensure that a supplier's products or services are planned, procured, processed, prepared, packaged, documented and delivered under controlled conditions to meet or exceed an agreed set of requirements. The result of a successful Certification programme will be consistent quality with reliable on time deliveries from the supplier.

The goals of Supplier Certification in the purchase of goods and services can be stated as follows:

- To maintain consistent quality in conformance with specification
- To improve quality over time
- To control processes rather than identify defects
- To control the cost of quality
- To support and optimise customers operations, for example assembly/productions
- To improve communications between supplier and customer
- To minimise lead-times (both external and internal)
- To remove inventory from the supply chain

### Supplier Certification Process

**Preliminary Stage**
Establish objectives

**Stage 1 – Supplier Selection**

**Stage 2 – Preparation for the Certification Audit**
Review quality performance gaps

**Stage 3 – Conducting the Certification Audit**
Technical/Commercial/Quality Management/Managerial

**Stage 4 – Review of Audit Findings & Corrective Action**

**Stage 5 – Certification complete with ongoing programme for improvement**

**Stage 6 – Periodic Audit to maintain Certification**

Evans, P (1998)

### The Supplier Quality Assurance Process

An overview of this process is provided below:

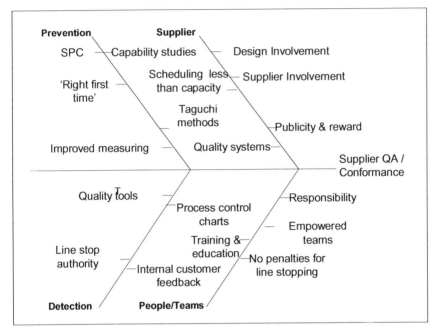

Ellison, H (2003)

## Checklist: The benefits of effective quality assurance

- Goods or services delivered within the agreed parameters to meet or exceed requirements
- Conformation to specification
- Control of processes rather than reaction to defects
- Minimisation of lead-times
- Hidden costs of quality identified
- Improved communication between supplier and customer
- Inventory reduction
- Facilitates joint cost reduction and benefits to supplier and customer

As a starting point, reviewing current practices is essential to identify hidden costs of quality and where duplication may exist with a supplier. This should include:

- Assessing inspection practices and looking for unnecessary or indiscriminate testing, backlogs of items awaiting inspection and goods held in quarantine.
- Reviewing performance measures and their effectiveness. For example, is the unit of measure (parts per million or percentage, say) sufficient to avoid a defect causing a

significant problem? Is the supplier actively engaged in solving the problem and is quality performance measures fed back to the supplier consistently?
- Evaluating the supplier's audit practices.
- Reviewing how the buyer organisation audits its supplier and what follow up action is taken.

A supplier quality assurance programme must form part of the overall supplier management strategy and the appropriate analysis applied before individual supplier are selected for implementation. Involving suppliers in the development of the relevant quality processes and ensuring implementation is focused on results will deliver significant value in not only preventing costly defects, but also in delivering opportunities for continuous improvement.

# The Strategic Supplier Development phase

The Strategic Supplier Development phase relates to those supplier development practices characterised by high levels of implementation complexity and buyer involvement with suppliers, therefore, requiring a greater use of company resources (personnel, time, and capital) than either the Reactive or Proactive Supplier Development phases.

Supplier development practices that have shown high levels of implementation complexity include training suppliers and involving suppliers in the buyer's new product design process. Supplier involvement in the buyer's design process is also linked to other supply practices, in particular, a collaborative atmosphere. A cooperative climate between suppliers and buyers can be achieved by intensive information exchanges such as suppliers releasing internal information (e.g. costs, quality levels) and buyers having access to a supplier's accounting and financial data. This type of communication with suppliers requires a high level of inter-organisation involvement and consequently we have included it in the Strategic Supplier Development phase.

In summary, the Strategic Supplier's Development phase therefore includes:

- Measures of training provided to suppliers.
- Supplier's involvement in the buyer's new product design process.
- Sharing of accounting information by the supplier.
- Sharing of cost and quality information by the supplier.

### Connections among supplier development activities
Sourcing from a limited number of suppliers can be the first step towards the implementation of more interactive and closer supply chain practices. This is because practices requiring closer interaction between buyer and supplier, such as involving the supplier in the product design process, are not feasible with a large supply base.

Supplier evaluation allows the buyer to identify what supplier performance indicators and/or capabilities need to be improved. Using this information enables the buyer to make a better decision about the kind of supplier development activity that needs to be implemented. For example, if the quality of materials needs to be improved, the buyer could collaborate directly with suppliers in materials improvement, or provide training on quality management to suppliers.

Similarly, if the focus is to improve on time delivery, the buyer could share production information with suppliers. Additionally, the reward and recognition of supplier performance improvements is not possible without continuous supplier performance evaluations. Supplier development activities are not independent, but complementary and, in some cases, they are a requisite for adopting other supplier development activities.

Procurement managers interested in enhancing Strategic Supplier Development practices such as providing training for suppliers, involvement in the buyer's product design process and sharing of confidential information with suppliers, would benefit most by adopting Proactive Supplier Development initiatives (e.g. rewarding and recognising supplier's performance improvements, visiting suppliers to assess their facilities, and collaborating with suppliers in materials improvement), as well as Reactive Supplier Development activities such as sourcing from a limited number of suppliers, supplier quality qualification, supplier performance evaluation and parts standardisation.

Such a cumulative response will be more effective in providing continuous improvement.

## Supply Base Strategies to maximise Supplier Performance

As we have seen above, there are many approaches are available to increase supplier performance contributions and capability improvements. The overall effect is that organisations pursue tactics which:

- Emphasise the direct and immediate improvement of supplier performance contribution towards a buying organisation's overall performance, and then possibly move on to:
- Focusing on the direct improvement of supplier capabilities which then increase supplier performance contributions more dramatically into the longer term.

We can further differentiate these approaches as those which move performance steadily along a conceptual supplier performance contribution, or capability improvement curve (the steady approaches), and those which actually shift the performance curve (the proactive approaches). Shifting the performance curve upward supports increased supplier performance contributions and capability improvements at an accelerate rate.

Certain strategy approaches have the potential, over time, to increase steadily supplier contributions and improvements. Examples of steady approaches to increase supplier performance contributions include:

- Electronic data interchange with suppliers.
- Longer term contracting with co-operative efforts.
- Supplier councils.
- Supplier rationalisation.

The viewpoint, for example, of Bournemouth Council, is that a long contract duration that does allow for performance to be monitored, managed and leveraged, with the relationship worked for the benefit of both parties, will win every time over short-term contracts.

# Developing and integrating local suppliers

The initial problems faced here by some organisations are that most of their local suppliers do not have the technological, resource and logistical capabilities that could support the organisations operation. However, by integrating local suppliers into the network and then working with them to develop selected product lines, it is possible for local suppliers to achieve a level of quality, cost, delivery and flexibility which can meet the company's immediate and long term needs.

One of the major reasons why the development of a partnership approach has been seen as unsuccessful with many assembly/production organisations; is that they expected and required suppliers to immediately supply them with parts on a just a time basis. It is important to allow such local suppliers the time to develop their operations to meet such new demand pressures.

The development of an effective supply chain is created through a strong working relationship being developed between the customer and its supplier. This relationship is aimed at developing its future technical and organisational capabilities, as well as providing advice and support towards ensuring product cost, flexibility and delivery reliability is achieved.

Some organisations have addressed the area of local supply chain development through a structured development programme. During this programme the selected local suppliers are initially termed associate suppliers. These 'associate' suppliers work alongside established suppliers and incrementally take on increased volumes of product as their technical and logistics capabilities increase. The development of the associate supplier approach is based on three major stages, namely:

1)      Technical development
2)      Capacity development
3)      Logistics development

Firstly, the technical capabilities of the company are developed prior to concentrating on their capacity and logistics capabilities.

The second stage of the development process aims at ensuring that the associate supplier can manufacture the products under the increasing volumes required to become a full supplier whilst maintaining product quality at every stage. For instance, the associate supplier will be given between 5 and 10 percent of the volume requirements of the established supplier in order to test its process capability and logistical capacity. Working with the process engineer, the company will be given increased product volumes as and when the system is capable of achieving the volumes under repeatable quality levels until the agreed capacity quota is reached for the company concerned. Finally, the third stage, the logistics system, is refined. What is particularly interesting is the ability to continually drive costs down year by year and to improve on the company's supply flexibility and delivery frequency. The company becomes a fully fledged company when the buying organisation is happy that there is suitable technical and logistics capacity within the company to allow for further expansion over successive years.

Below is a summary diagram of a structured supplier development approach for local suppliers follows:

**Supplier Development Methodology for local suppliers**

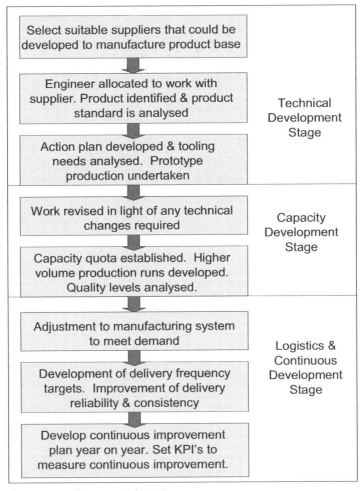

Thomas, A and Barton, R (2007)

# Increasing Supplier Performance

Successful implementation of proactive procurement approaches can accelerate supplier performance contributions and capability improvements in a shorter period of time, compared to the use of steady or traditional approaches. Given the importance of suppliers along with their limited performance improvement response over time, senior management must take action that is proactive and direct to improve supplier contributions and capability improvements. Supplier's performance can be improved as shown below:

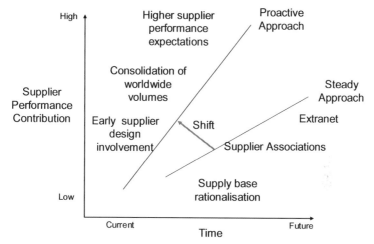

**After** Monczka, R.M and Trent, R.J and Callaghan, T.J (1993)

Examples of steady approaches to improve supplier capabilities include:

- Setting higher supplier capability objectives.
- Statistical process control (SPC).
- Supplier certification.
- Formal education and training programmes.

Each of these activities, when carried out properly, can increase supplier contributions and improvements at a relatively steady rate over time. The supplier's capability will be improved, as shown below:

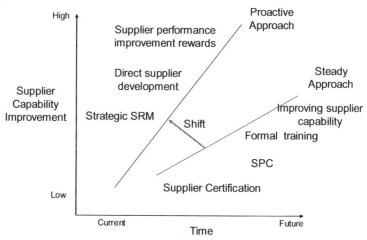

**After** Monczka, R.M and Trent, R.J and Callaghan, T.J (1993)

139

Many organisations have yet to realise the total performance contributions that a world-class supply base can provide. For an organisation to develop a competitive advantage from its sourcing process and its suppliers, it must take more strategic actions that focus specifically on increasing supplier performance contributions.

Purchasers must also begin to challenge proactively and increase the performance expectations of suppliers. This recognises that increased supplier performance directly affects a buying organisation's competitive position. By proactively increasing supplier performance expectations, a buying organisation expects supplier contributions to increase at an accelerated rate. Eventually, organisations must maintain only those suppliers capable of satisfying higher performance expectation levels.

## Case Study: Motorola

Suppliers must satisfy stringent performance expectations in at least four critical areas. These include:

- Keeping pace in attaining perfect quality
- Remaining on the leading edge of technology
- Practicing just in time manufacturing and delivery
- Offering a cost competitive service

### Consolidation of purchase volume

The objective of purchase volume consolidation is to maximise an organisations buying leverage. The end result should be not only lower purchase prices for commonly purchased items but also the selection of suppliers which provide consistent world class quality, delivery and support to each buying location. Consolidation can involve combining separate purchase agreements for the same supplier into a single, larger volume agreement or eliminating multiple suppliers of a common item by establishing a single company wide source.

### Worldwide co-ordination of purchase strategy

Systematic co-ordination of procurement strategy can also increase a supplier's performance contributions. This approach requires procurement centres or business units located throughout different geographic regions to develop jointly regional or worldwide procurement strategies that maximise the total contributions of best in class suppliers.

Traditionally, many manufacturers have decentralised the materials and production function to the division or business unit level. While this may contribute to procurement responsiveness, it also contributes to inefficiency and lost opportunities. Uncoordinated procurement strategy results in lost purchase leverage opportunities worldwide. It also lowers an organisations overall procurement effectiveness as they are not able to share material expertise between buying units.

Organisations can benefit directly from the coordination of procurement strategy, product design, supplier performance information, suppliers, and common purchased items between business units or procurement centres. Worldwide integration and coordination represents a proactive and more strategic approach to accelerated supplier performance contribution because organisations coordinate and manage supply base strategies at a highly visible, executive level. Additionally, the procurement function, usually through cross functional sourcing teams, searches for the best suppliers world wide to provide common purchased times or families of items.

### Early and continuous supplier design involvement and selection

Early supplier design involvement and selection requires key suppliers to participate at the concept or pre-design phase of new product development. Supplier involvement may be informal, although the supplier may already have a purchase contract for production of an item. Early involvement will increasingly be through participation on cross-functional product development teams.

Early involvement recognises that qualified suppliers have more to offer a buying organisation than the basic production of an item according to established specifications. Early supplier design involvement, part of a simultaneous engineering approach between buyer and seller, seeks to maximise the benefit received from a supplier's engineering, design, testing, manufacturing, and tooling capabilities. It can also help ensure that suppliers can reliably produce a designed part with existing processes.

This approach represents a direct effort to reduce total product development cycle time by using key suppliers early in the design process.

Some organisations have yet to develop a closer, trusting relationship with their suppliers and also do not have the appropriate confidentiality agreements to maximise the benefit of early supplier involvement. Greater trust and commitment between buyer and seller, however, has always been a stated goal of the supplier rationalisation process.

# Direct supplier development

Direct supplier development involves the commitment of resources by the buying unit for the improvement of an existing supplier capability, or, the development of new performance capability. Direct support can involve providing capital, equipment, technology, or the assignment of support personnel to a supplier's facility. This differs from indirect supplier development that stresses supplier encouragement, training, and self-improvement.

Direct supplier development efforts are critical for effective supply base management. Once a company reduces its supply base and assures itself that it has best in world suppliers, supply base improvements will occur primarily through the development of existing supplier capabilities and not through large-scale supplier switching.

Often organisations develop supplier capabilities primarily through increased supplier performance goals and formal education and training programmes. Many organisations stress these two activities are overwhelmingly beneficial, over the more direct activities of providing support personnel, capital, equipment, technology or, the direct involvement with suppliers in identifying and eliminating non value added costs, processes and time. The actions required to accelerate supplier capability improvements, however, are those emphasised the least, for example, providing personnel, capital, and equipment resources to accelerate development with resulting preferential treatment expected from the supplier.

An example of a systematic supplier development effort is Toyota and Nissan; who send teams of engineers directly to suppliers to help adopt lean and efficient production methods. The programme is open to suppliers of all types of purchased materials that can benefit from direct assistance.

## Checklist: Ranking for Developing supplier capabilities

1. Increase supplier performance goals
2. Conduct education and training programmes
3. Provide technology
4. Provide support personnel
5. Provide equipment
6. Provide capital

Such supplier development requires a mutual recognition by the buyer and the seller of the need for continuous performance improvement. Executive management at the buying unit must commit the time, personnel and financial resources to support the suppliers who are willing to participate.

A successful programme requires a proactive attitude that moves well beyond increased supplier performance goals and education and training programmes. This approach, however, requires very close monitoring of the supplier development effort, as well as of each supplier's actual improvement over time.

The need to develop, maintain and manage a supply base, which performs at world-class levels, must not only be of interest to functional procurement management. Indeed, management must begin to link closely corporate/business unit, product and procurement strategy. The ability to compete rests, in part, on the development of proactive strategies which recognise the critical contributions of procurement and the supply base towards achieving over all corporate objectives.

Besides recognising the critical role of procurement during the development of corporate/business unit and product strategy, management must take other steps to maximise procurement performance contribution. Only by working with suppliers can a company hope to remain at the forefront of technology and hence protect its share of the market.

### Supplier Co-ordination and Associations

Kyoryoku-Kai or "Supplier Association" is a concept which was first developed in Japan, and uses study groups where new production techniques can be learnt, such as Lean and/or Agile Supply, Statistical Process Control, Just in Time delivery, Value Analysis, and Sustainability techniques. Essentially such supplier co-ordination is a technique to add value as well as remove waste. It involves buyers identifying its most important suppliers and bringing them together on a regular basis for the purpose of mutual benefit and in particular to:

- To devolve strategy and policy throughout the chain to create a sense of common purpose.
- To strengthen trust and the relationships of the members.
- To share knowledge and expertise.
- To facilitate joint development and learning.
- To jointly identify ways of minimising waste.

The process of learning for member suppliers does not merely depend on technology transfer from the client company to its suppliers, but also on mutual teaching among member suppliers. This might be through mutual factory visits, to offer constructive criticisms and suggestions on factory layout, process technology, or quality control procedures; all of which tend to lead to enhanced efficiency and effectiveness.

It is important to select suppliers that are in synergy with each other as there would be little point in the selecting suppliers if there were no inter-relationship between them. This means that suppliers should be grouped into categories in which they have something in common, e.g. a glass bottle supplier, a bottle top supplier, and a packaging supplier. Another way of grouping would be into supply chains so that the first, second and third tier suppliers of a vital supply chain can be brought together for the supplier co-ordination and mutual benefit.

Trust is absolutely critical to the success of kyoryoku kai, between all those participating. In some cases it may be necessary to have confidentiality agreements in place. Additionally, all suppliers must be able to benefit from kyoryoku kai. The buying organisation must ensure that they do so; otherwise the forum will not be sustainable. Ideally, the forum should be a long-term arrangement with the objective of continuous improvement.

There are alternatives to kyoryoku kai that can achieve similar ends – such as an eSupply Hub which is a virtual meeting place in which suppliers can air issues, and share experiences and problems. However, kyoryoku kai is a way of solving problems and bringing about improvements but procurement and supply chain management professionals need to deploy the necessary hard and soft skills to determine whether, or when, circumstances are right to ensure success.

**Supplier Development Positioning Matrix and Model**
Another range of supplier development approaches is given overleaf:

143

| Supplier | Criteria | | Strategy |
|---|---|---|---|
| To provide mutual competitive advantage | Maximum network benefits | Stage 4 | Network Development |
| To improve continually technical / competitive advantage | Maximum mutual benefit | Stage 3 | Systematic Development Programme |
| Supply goods customer does not want to make | Lowest cost | Stage 2 | Reactive Problem Solving |
| Supply goods customer does not make | Lowest price | Stage 1 | External Accreditation |

**After:** Hines, James & Jones (1995) Supplier Development Positioning Matrix

Again we see the gradual progression towards greater co-ordination of supply chain networks and systematic supplier developments programmes, to give greater mutual advantage to buyers and suppliers.

This is further confirmed in the model by Massey and McCartney below:

# Checklist: Supplier Development Model

| Stage 1 Individual | • Cheapest price<br>• No TCO<br>• Little performance monitoring<br>• Short term relationships |
|---|---|
| Stage 2 Fragmented | • Vendor rating<br>• Lack of supplier information<br>• Short term focus<br>• Vision is not communicated |
| Stage 3 Integrated | • Cross functional teams<br>• Policy communicated to suppliers<br>• Jointly agreed KPIs<br>• Open communication<br>• Risk sharing |
| Stage 4 Networked | • Supplier associations (Kyoryoku kai)<br>• Kaizen<br>• Trust<br>• Shared information<br>• Aligned processes |

**After** Massey L and McCartney L (1998)

## Longer-term deals are better than shorter contracts

More than three quarters of buyers prefer long-term contracts with suppliers, according to a Supply Management poll. The survey of 100 buyers found 83 percent in favour of longer-term relationships, while 17 percent preferred shorter deals. Most respondents said providing contracts are maintained and managed properly, having longer-term relationships with suppliers is beneficial to both parties.

### Case Studies: Long term contracts

**Tetley**
Tetley believe the benefits of long-term contracts include "price and supply stability, the ability to get the supplier properly tuned into their needs and for Tetley to tune in to their strengths, and the ability to develop products, services or systems".

**Kronospan**
Believe long term contracts have greater rewards, and that they "encourage suppliers to provide added value initiatives and ideas that may produce greater cost reductions, not just short term price reductions that result from constantly changing suppliers and contracts".

# Part four: Summary

- Supplier development is the process of working with certain suppliers on a one to one basis to improve their performance for the benefit of the buying organisation.
- There are very good and sound reasons for embarking on a supplier development process and these are as follows:
    - Improving supplier performance
    - Reducing costs
    - Resolving serious quality issues
    - Developing new routes to supply
    - Improving business alignment between the supplier and the buying organisation
    - Developing a product or service not currently available in the market place
    - Generating competition for a high price product or service dominating the market place

There are three supplier development factors to be considered, which are direct involvement, incentives and enforced competition.

- Direct involvement includes such practices as formal evaluation of the suppliers, supplier certification, site visits, supplier recognition, feedback to suppliers, training, information evaluation of suppliers, inviting supplier's personnel to the organisation's facilities, and verbal or written requests to improve performance.

- The incentives factor includes the promise of current and future benefits to the supplier if performance was improved.
- Enforced competition includes using two or three suppliers per purchased item.

The key phases of supplier development are as follows:

- The Reactive Supplier Development phase relates to those supplier development practices that require the most limited organisation involvement and minimum investment of the company's resources (i.e. personnel, time and capital) and thus, are likely to be implemented first in an effort to improve supplier performance and/or capabilities.
- The Proactive Supplier Development phase refers to supplier development practices characterised by increased yet still moderate levels of procurement involvement and implementation complexity, therefore requiring comparatively more company resources (personnel, time and capital) than the Reactive Supplier Development phase.
- The Strategic Supplier Development phase relates to those supplier development practices characterised by high levels of implementation complexity and buyer involvement with suppliers, therefore, requiring a greater use of company resources (personnel, time, and capital) than either the Reactive or Proactive Supplier Development phases.

# Part five: Supplier Management: Making the change

There are important aspects to be considered when thinking about introducing supplier management. Clearly, some of these have already been considered. However, here we shall be examining this in more detail.

## Supply Chain Information Sharing

An effective supply chain requires a smoothly operating information system, in which accurate information flows among the links in a timely, coordinated fashion, minimising distortion. The system must incorporate supply and demand information, and constantly changing information about real world events that affect the chain. Information flows can be rationalised and streamlined, with feedback loops defined to measure performance, both uni-directionally and two-way.

In a supply chain, goods can flow through a very complex series of plants, intermediaries, warehouses and distribution centres, and the flow can involve multiple modes of transport. Organisations increasingly view effective supply chain management as an important contributor to a company's overall competitiveness. Structured information management therefore lies at the heart of supply chain management and for the many components of supply chain to work effectively, their activities must be coordinated and synchronized carefully.

By focusing attention on a company's primary data flows, the company may improve the overall reliability of the chain and may develop metrics to aid in reducing distortions. A problem however, is ensuring the timely, coordinated receipt of information by all relevant parties.

### Transparency
Managing supply relationships needs some form of shared risk or two-way transparency. This means that, to get reliable and useful information from the supplier, the customer has to share knowledge on its own operations. This can only be done where the exchange is justifiable and acceptable for both parties.

To develop transparency means moving to situations in which the customer allows the supplier to understand the customer's own operations and provide specific help. This means mapping the relationship as an area of jointly owned operations, within which both parties employ assets, incur costs and expect returns. Requests for information must be justified, explaining why the information is needed and sharing must be selective. It requires two-way sharing, trust and respect, because sensitive data is being exchanged.

Cisco Systems, for example, discusses operating details with its suppliers, giving extensive access to its information systems to develop mutual business benefits. In each case the benefits are reduced costs and improved success for both parties. Open book approaches have been used for some time now, however these are considered by some to be a one-way approach, as whilst the supplier offers sensitive information; no information is shared with them.

Some of the key similarities and differences between a traditional open-book approach and a transparent relationship can be seen as follows:

| Open Book Relationships | Transparent Relationships |
|---|---|
| **One Way** – the customer requires sensitive information, like costs, from the supplier, but gives nothing, except scheduling data, in return | **Two Way** – customer and supplier exchange sensitive data |
| **Carte Blanche** – supplier reveals all costs. No justification is given. | **Specific** – information requests are justified to both parties' satisfaction. |
| **Supplier's Risk** – all risk is with the supplier and the customer risks nothing | **Focused** – the whole point is to address a specific opportunity to reduce costs, times and waste |
| **Unbalanced benefits** – the customer gets lower prices and the supplier might keep business | **Sharing risk** – both parties open their books, as far as necessary |
| **Flawed** – the supplier can change any sensitive data to hedge any risk to them | **Potentially sound** – less reason for either party to cheat as they are both sharing sensitive data |
| **Crude** – naïve use of economic power by the customer, matched by a risk premium in the supplier's costs | **Pragmatic** – based on "trust and verify" |
| **Subject to 'spin'** – there is talk of "trusting" each other, but often there is little evidence of it | **Potentially cost effective** – avoiding the costs that arise when simple power is used |
| **Adversarial** – part of the redundant paradigm of overt conflict | **New role** – potentially a new strategic role for procurement and supply |
| **Inefficient** – potentially adds costs to the supply chain | **Challenging** – part of a radical departure to collaborative, lean supply |

**After Lamming, R, Harrison, D, Caldwell, N, (2000)**

# Case Study – British Nuclear Group

British Nuclear Group supply network innovation programme (SNIP) has been designed to introduce some of the principles of transparency into its procurement, and it is already reaping dividends.

"Suppliers are not there to be told what to do, they're there to share ideas and stimulate innovation."

For many years, employees have worn disposable plastic suits for work in radioactive environments, but managers began to feel that improvements needed to be made, especially for welders. Its supplier was already working on a range of modifications, so the two combined forces and developed a new suit together. The review was so wide ranging that the supplier even moved to a different sub contractor and produced a suite that was tougher, more flexible and simpler to dispose of than the previous work wears.

**Information sharing, supplier development and performance**
Organisations that wish to enhance product quality, cut costs, improve flexibility and shorten lead-times have concentrated their efforts on effectively managing their supply chains. One of the critical requirements of effective supply chain management, as mentioned earlier, is the creation of a synchronized flow of materials and information from suppliers to their customer. However, finding suppliers already organised to meet a buyer's requirements for quality, delivery, flexibility and cost reductions is likely to be a challenge. One effective way buying organisations can meet this challenge is by developing their suppliers in ways that improve suppliers' capabilities.

The need to improve supplier's quality and delivery performance while at the same time, reducing the costs of supplied materials and parts, has motivated buyers to engage in supplier development activities. One of the most frequently cited activities is the provision of technical support to key suppliers. This technical support might consist of direct investment in equipment and personnel in suppliers, evaluation of supplier performance and sharing feedback on the evaluation results, visiting supplier's plants and supplier certification. The ultimate purpose of providing technical support to suppliers is to reduce a buyer's transaction costs through improved supplier performance. Such supplier development support includes such activities as:

- Investing in suppliers' equipment or personnel
- Providing technical expertise
- Evaluating suppliers' operations
- Offering feedback

It is argued that suppliers and buyers interact more frequently when they use information technology because information technology facilitates the communication.

**Information sharing with organisations**
Information sharing within an organisation should precede the information sharing between organisations and supplier development support. Information sharing within an organisation is necessary for helping organisation members to identify critical issues regarding their suppliers. It is also common practice to use cross-functional teams comprised of members from internal functions such as procurement, marketing and production to solve supplier quality problems. Thus, information sharing within the organisation becomes a coordinating mechanism for promoting the teamwork.

It has been seen that a potential supplier's willingness to share information is one of the key criteria in Japanese automakers' selection of their suppliers. Empirical research results show that organisations successful in supplier development effectively share information, in a timely manner and frequently, with their suppliers. Effective information sharing of buyer requirements increases understanding of both suppliers and buyers and results in a more committed relationship on the part of the suppliers. It was also found that buying organisations committed to supplier development are more apt to share information about product use, predicted future requirements and proprietary information than are organisations not involved in supplier development.

Good relationships with suppliers improve the quality of the buyer's products by enabling suppliers to become involved early in the buying organisation's design of products/services. If they work with cross functional product development teams, suppliers can assist purchasers in choosing materials and parts that can be produced most efficiently. If they are involved early, suppliers can also offer suggestions regarding product and/or component simplification. It would seem reasonable, then, to expect that early supplier involvement in the buying organisation's design of products/services, in the ways discussed above, will help buyers design quality into their products and thereby improve them.

# Supplier support

Empirical evidence indicates that supplier support has positive effects on both a buyer's product quality and financial performance. The main objective of supplier development activities is improving supplier performance. These activities require that a buying organisation invest time and resources in suppliers, if they are to significantly reduce incoming defects, increase the percent of on-time delivery, reduce order cycle times and increase the percent or orders received complete.

It is not uncommon for buyers to teach their suppliers' employees quality improvement skills or educate them on such topics as statistical process control and total quality management. By evaluating suppliers' performance and providing feedback, buying organisations can train and educate suppliers to fix problems that are hurting the suppliers' performance.

Empirical studies show that support activities, result in improved buyer supplier performance and enhanced product/service quality of the buying organisation. Moreover, as the literature shows, supplier support is often associated with supply base reduction, and the most important benefit of a smaller supply base is improved product quality for buyers.

Supplier support also results in reduced cost for a buying organisation's products and services. Enhanced delivery performance of suppliers and improved quality of incoming materials and parts eliminate interruptions in the production process. Further, improved quality and timely delivery of supplied materials allow buyers to receive incoming materials only in immediately required quantities, thereby eliminating the need for safety stocks and reducing inventory carrying costs.

Some organisations are however reactive in supplier development efforts, meaning that they attempt to develop their suppliers after a problem actually occurs. In contrast, organisations wanting to create a first rate supply base that can provide a competitive edge over the long term adopt a proactive approach; they identify crucial commodities and the suppliers of them that require development.

In a poll of Supply & Demand Chain Executive's (2005) readers, sharing information and collaborating with trading partners was rated as a company's top challenge. Further studies on measuring supply chain practices identify communication/information sharing and supplier partnerships as important factors of Supply Chain Management.

The options available for supplier support are as follows:
- Provision of technical support (e.g. invests in equipment or personnel) to help key supplier to improve their operations.
- Provide technical expertise to help fix problems on supplier's production line.
- Employees evaluate key supplier's operations and provide feedback to help them to improve.
- Employees work with key supplier's employees to improve their operations.

All parties must have the best data for scrutinising supply chain performance to take out hidden costs, such as waste in the form of unnecessarily high levels of stock, duplication of suppliers and processes, and poorly planned logistics.

As the scope for tightening up these elements decreases, innovation among partners rises in importance. Partnering has always insisted that everyone understand the importance of innovation for maintaining a competitive edge, especially as supply chain costs rise and waste is eliminated.

Buyers must have more data concerning suppliers business and they must also let their suppliers know more about their own organisations' business.

## Case Study: Siemens UK

Siemens cut millions of pounds from its supply costs by getting to grips with its supplier relationship management process.

Suppliers are arguably the most important contributors to competitive advantage, helping organisations not only to reduce costs, but also encourage innovation. There is a huge amount of new ideas that you can bring in from suppliers.

Underpinning good supplier relations is good management that involves selecting, evaluating, classifying and then developing suppliers.

### Critical evaluation
Supplier evaluation is central for the electronics company. Introduced initially in Germany and Switzerland, the process has now been introduced to the UK's corporate shared service division.

While not the division's first encounter with supplier management, it's more rigorous approach is expected to yield dramatic improvements by reducing costs in the supply chain and improving relationships and service. Ultimately it aims to generate an estimated two million pounds worth of savings initially.

They invited suppliers to quarterly review meetings, but didn't have the information to back up their comments on their performance. Most of what they had was subjective; there were no hard facts behind it.

Without concrete information, the division could not communicate its expectations to suppliers.

### Monitoring performance

First, the evaluation tool logs performance and feedback about its existing suppliers. Siemens then presents this information to them, highlighting areas of good and poor performance. This generates one of two responses; either encouraging an improvement in the relationship, or justifying a decision to end it.

The evaluation happens at least once a year and suppliers are assessed against four criteria:

- Procurement
- Quality
- Logistics
- Technology

Each assessment varies according to the commodity. And criteria sets are weighted. Individual suppliers are awarded points for total cost performance, cost reduction, fulfilment of strategic requirements and co-operation, service and support.

Following the evaluation process, suppliers are awarded poor, insufficient, good or outstanding status. This is an important element of supplier management, as "once you evaluate suppliers' performance you can start discussions about problem areas and look at how they can improve and develop".

Based on the gaps identified in the evaluation, Siemens sets performance improvement objectives. Suppliers are invited to quarterly review meetings to ensure they continue to improve and also prevent and discuss any issues.

Another element to Siemens' approach is supplier aided economic value-added (SAEVA) process developed last year by the company's UK procurement division. Here, suppliers are encouraged to deliver improvements that result in savings. Through this method Siemens has cut several more million pounds from its supply bills. Suppliers are thankful for feedback that is transparent and objective. It also becomes easier to talk about issues.

### Share responsibility

The supplier evaluation tool also enables strategic procurement and logistics, together with internal customers, to share responsibility for supplier management. First, procurement builds the evaluation and agrees the questions with suppliers. These are then distributed to the customers who use the procured goods and services.

While the buying department will answer the procurement questions, issues covering quality, logistics and technology will be completed by other departments.

The evaluation part takes about six weeks annually but the entire supplier management process takes a whole year.

There are also plans to introduce a classification tool. As well as monitoring the supplier's past performance, it will examine the supplier's fit with Siemens on going plans. Suppliers are evaluated here in terms of how they fit with those plans, in terms of market factors and commitment, their competitiveness and their technology.

# Added value of Relationships

Research organisation Grasp concluded that UK organisations risk both their reputation and their financial stability because they do not know enough about their suppliers. Good relationships help organisations mitigate risks when they fall on hard times, and need to audit their supply chains or seek innovation. Traditionally, procurement has been too cost-centric, commentators say, and there is only so far purchasers can go in driving down the price of a product.

The focus on cost is shortsighted, whereas successful business relationships should be mutual and collaborative, because added value and cost savings are realised only, after the time and effort is put into establishing and nurturing such relationships. For example, Siemens had saved more than one million pounds in one category in 18 months after encouraging a supplier to come up with money saving ideas. Pharmaceutical organisation Astra Zeneca reviewed its suppliers' financial information to ensure they continue to be sustainable and says it has achieved time and cost savings by working closely with them.

Relationships do not have to be fully-fledged partnerships to be beneficial, as long as both parties know where they stand. The key is communications of expectations, unfortunately however, some buyers choose instead, to over use aggression, leverage and power.

**Contract management systems**
Electronic contract management systems are making it easier for organisations to manage suppliers. Whilst many organisations have invested heavily in systems and processes to find the best price or supplier of goods and services, so far many have paid little attention to the management of the contracts after they have been signed and sealed. Many can recall instances when contracts are, at best, filed in locked cabinets or at worst kept in a manager's drawer and eventually but assuredly lost.

**Central Systems**
US organisations, under pressure from Sarbanes-Oxley (SOX) legislation to show appropriate controls and processes for all contract negotiations, have done rather better than their UK counterparts.

They have invested in software, from around a dozen vendors, that stores all contracts centrally and sends out an alert when they are due for renewal. It allows organisations to search scanned versions of old contracts, and to create new ones electronically. Final versions are still printed and signed with pen and ink, but since they are also held electronically they can be collected, stored and checked with more ease.

The most expensive electronic contract management systems (ECMS) are often integrated into back end purchase to pay systems, allowing an organisation to match contract terms with the goods or services delivered. Cheaper systems will run a document "repository" or store, with reminders of renewal dates but fewer links to financial systems.

Contract management products will go a long way to solving the biggest hurdle; making sure that all the organisation's contracts are in one place, and can be searched easily and quickly. Equally important are automated systems that help procurement managers create new contracts from a series of pull down templates, previously approved by the legal department. There are products that will add clauses to a contact automatically, depending on its type and the standard payment terms.

Network Rail uses Oracle's contract management system to help it set up complicated contracts where technical experts, project delivery managers and in house lawyers can all work with one version. Organisations can generate huge numbers of contracts. Emptoris, a contract management supplier, has a healthcare client with 250,000 contracts in its system, many of them up to 60 pages long.

# Collaboration

Some large retailers and manufacturers have spent years analyzing each other's forecasts in a bid to guess production and demand. However, a few are now starting to focus on building open relationships and sharing the benefits of each other's input, from the end of the production line through to the point of purchase. The key to success here lies with everyone being given the opportunity to understand and influence the factors that drive supply chain activity and in this retail example, this essentially means empowering manufacturers to do everything a retailer does, representing a shared ownership of the consumer. In other words, total visibility of each other's business, open and trusting relationships and sharing everything from planning production to the technology for planning promotions in stores.

In this regard James Hulse, Iceland's supplier development manager, comments: *"Suppliers rarely have sight of their products once they leave their factories, so we needed to give them a line of sight into the business. Getting forecasts wrong can and does lead to significant cases of overstock. By allowing our suppliers to get more involved in the entire supply chain, we knew we could benefit from few stock-outs, improved availability, more successful promotions and, ultimately, better customer service."*

*"The payback has been quick which has made the investment required definitely worth it. Every supplier tells us that trading relationships have improved dramatically. And it's not just the financial return, it's also the soft benefits that everyone is talking about, such as being able to plan promotions more effectively and working more efficiently together."*
**Logistics Manager, June 2004**

Key retail players in the convenience sector have already had tremendous success in building these types of collaborative relationships with numerous suppliers across major brands and own label manufacturers. The reported benefits include:

- Vastly reduced supply chain costs.
- More efficient procurement of raw materials.
- Improved manufacture planning.
- Increased sales through raised on shelf availability.
- Better working relationships.

It is clear, therefore, that collaboration and trust are needed for effective supplier management. However this can mean that a totally different approach is needed; a point well noted by Bill Knittle, (Global Procurement, Director of refining and marketing in BP), whereby *"Relationship management skills are a totally different skill-set. Don't expect anyone trained only to be aggressive for 20 years to be good at this..."*
**Supply Management, 28 February 2008**

Collaboration may also run counter to those who have beliefs of procurement and contracting being all about "squeezing suppliers" and also to those who display an adversarial approach. For example:

*"There is no doubt in the days of Rail track (Network Rail's predecessor) that it was highly adversarial. It has been changing ever since. We are not quite in a fully cooperative environment but are moving in the right direction."*
**Supply Management, 8 May 2008, Network Rail to improve its supplier relationships**

*"The big boys in the construction industry tend to treat suppliers as if they're muck on their shoes"*
**Supply Management, 13 March 2008, Barratt homes repay £19K to supplier**

We will continue by discussing why a collaborative approach is so often needed.

## Supply chain and competitive advantage

The eminent UK Supply Chain academic, Professor Martin Christopher noted in the early 1990s that *"The future is one not of competing organisations but of competing supply chains."*

Therefore, success in the future, comes from how we manage our supply chains; however, to do this to do this we will need to have a "collaborative advantage".

Despite this, 'there may be trouble ahead', as the UK's Professor Alan Waller has noted:
*"The supply chain lies no longer with an individual company; we have global net works cutting across countries and organisations. The only way forward is to get players working to a common agenda - the collaboration agenda. We have been taught to compete: nobody has taught us to work together. The need and awareness is there but still nobody has taught us how to do it"'.*

The fundamental issue here is that Supply Chain Management is about how we are able to "Integrate, coordinate and control the Supply Chain". However, this integration and coordination is also needed "in the hearts and minds of people" and not just by using technical tools/systems/techniques.

The importance of people has been usefully noted by the master management guru Peter Drucker, who noted: *"Because the object of management is a human community held together by the work bond for a common purpose, management always deals with the nature of man".*

The real competition, therefore, in most organisations these days comes not just from organisations competing against each other, but increasingly comes from competing supply chains. There is also a growing approach to maximise benefits from all of the supply chain and to go beyond the first level suppliers.

Competitive advantage is to found by doing things better or by doing thing cheaper. Looking for these advantages really means extending from within a company, towards, their supply chains. This means looking to remove sub functional conflicts from all the interdependent processes, whether these processes are internal or external to a business. Accordingly, it is the supply chain that can now provide the competitive advantage for a business.

## Supply chain structures and benefits

The way the supply chain is structured and managed is, therefore, critical. Some reported benefits of following a supply chain approach follow; it will be noted that different approaches give different results:

|  | No Supply Chain: Functional Silos | Internal Integrated Supply Chain | Plus, External Integration to The first level only |
|---|---|---|---|
| Inventory days of supply Indexed | 100 | 78 | 62 |
| Inventory carrying cost % sales | 3.2% | 2.1% | 1.5% |
| On time in Full deliveries | 80% | 91% | 95% |
| Profit % Sales | 8% | 11% | 14% |

To get these benefits, organisations will need to more away from a functional silo approach and who leads the internal integrated supply chain will be a critical decision for each organisation to make. However, it will be seen that with a supply chain integrated approach, inventory costs do fall, while profit and the service fulfilment do increase. This represents the "best of both worlds" for any organisation undertaking the approach.

156

Additional benefits from supply chain management will only usually come when there is a joint examination of all costs/service levels with all the players; to then obtain the reduced lead-times and improved total costs/service for all parties in the network. This means going beyond the first tier of suppliers and looking also at the suppliers' supplier and so on. To undertake such an extended view of the supply chain may well require a total Supply Chain Re-thinking; a topic addressed more fully in *"Excellence in Supply Chain Management"*.

However, as clearly shown above, working and collaborating fully with all players in the Supply Chain is the only way to find the optimum/ideal cost/service balance.

# Trust

Collaboration involves trust and there are different levels of trust; three levels of trust have been usefully identified as follows:
1) Trust Level one, Contractual and "Service":
- Boundary time bound trust for standard performance.
- Exchanged data for transactions.

2) Trust Level two, Competence and "Satisfaction":
- Reliable trust for satisfactory performance.
- Some information sharing and cooperation.

3) Trust Level three, Commitment and "Success":
- Goodwill open ended trust giving beyond expectations success.
- Cognitive connected decision making.
(**Source:** After Dr. Mari Sako)

These levels are expanded below:

| Level one trust | Level two trust | Level three trust |
|---|---|---|
| Boundary trust | Reliable trust | Goodwill trust |
| Contractual | Competence | Commitment |
| Explicit promises | Known standards | Anything that is required to foster the relationship |
| Standard performance | Satisfactory performance | Success beyond expectation |
| Mistakes bring enforcement | ⟹ | Mistakes give shared learning for advantage |
| Exchange data for transactions | Cooperate on information for mutual access | Cognitive connections and joint decision making |
| Animal brain | ⟹ | Human brain |
| Symbonic | Share | Swap |
| Time bound (as far as the contract says) | ⟹ | Open-ended, ongoing and leaving a legacy |

**Lessons from experience on trust (the "T" word):**
- *"It changes the paradigm. It's definitely a different type of relationship with your customer. It's based on mutual trust and it's got to be there to succeed".*

157

- *"On paper, the process seems simple to implement, but in the real world of personalities and professional relationships, there are many obstacles to climb. Trust is very important for success".*
- *"You can define any relationship by the degree of trust. No trust = no relationship. This applies both in business and also in personal life".*
- *"The biggest thing my boss could do for me is to trust me."*

Trust is fundamentally about "having to give up, to another, what you personally believe is valuable to you", it is "one for all and all for one" and it is a "willing interdependence." Trust is built when behaviour matches expectations. It involves consistency in motives and in accountability for actions; therefore trust becomes a self-fulfilling prophecy. Trust is firstly built between people, one on one, and is not something that is built remotely, between organisational departments or external organisations. Fortunately, trust can be won by consistently telling the truth in a way that others can verify. Trust is about transparency and includes the admission of mistakes, and not covering them up.

Building trust is a "one on one" job; this is the foundational building block from which trust can develop. It will involve the following:

- Doing what you say you will do.
- Going beyond conventional expectations.
- Undertaking open and honest communicating.
- Being patient.
- Accepting and admitting to mistakes.
- Ensuring the other party gets a fair outcome.

Trust, due to its emotional roots, can defy logic. Some people trust straight away with no real basis (this is a good thing, as this is one of the primary bases for society and community). Some people will need to see repeated behaviour before they will trust. Others will need consistency in behaviour for months or years. Some, however, will never trust.

Trust does have a critical and sound logic aspect; trust reduces uncertainty. There is no second-guessing: what they say is true, commitments are honoured and therefore bargaining, monitoring, handling disputes should be minimised.

| Trust is | Trust is not |
|---|---|
| Confidence in own and others abilities | Blind faith in the unknown |
| Experienced by working together with integrity, honesty and openness | Cheap, as there is high cost of failure. Sometimes failure is critical |
| A positive power using both the heart and the head | A single "my" view |
| Learning and being flexible and willing to change | Formal rules |
| Tough and confronting without being confrontational, as expectations have to be met | Easy |
| Bonding, intimacy and working together face/face | Keeping your distance |
| Visible leadership | Invisible leadership |
| A genuine belief system that sees it is the right thing to do as all will benefit | Used temporary or short term or for single benefit |

**How to Build Trust**

Be non-judgmental

Be open:
- Initiate self – disclosure; reveal your thinking and feelings
- Volunteer information
- Reveal your values and priorities

Be congruent and honest:
- Say what you think; state your opinion, even when different from others
- State your wants and needs
- Encourage honesty in others
- State clearly what you will and will not reveal

Be reliable:
- Do what you say you will do
- Set clear and realistic limits on both sides
- Treat commitments seriously and develop reliable processes

Be a striver for continuous improvement:
- Influence your organisation to create more mutual benefit for the relationships
- Exchange candid feedback on how well the relationship is working

And finally
- All parties must come to believe that the others will do what they have said they will do.
- All parties must find a way to be comfortable with the risk of being open and vulnerable to the others, in the secure belief that the other party will not take unfair advantage.
- All must show willingness to help the others become more successful.
- Broken agreements destroy trust and lead to bad implementations and performance.
- Continuous improvement is the fabric and product of trust in a relationship.

A final word here from Sir John Harvey Jones: *"Teams can only work together if they trust and trust requires mutuality of respect, integrity, and mutuality of regard."*

# Soft skills are the hard skills to acquire

Changing from more transactional methods to collaborative approaches goes far beyond the technical issues, of, for example, ICT connectivity, and fully embraces the soft skills. The view and belief here from sponsors of collaborative approaches is that if all players would work well together, a lot more would get done more efficiently and more effectively. It is seen that the evidence for this from relationship principles is overwhelming.

However, many people will not subscribe to such a mutually sharing collaborative management approach. A major reason for not doing this, is when people believe that procurement and business generally is founded on power plays, for example, across the buying activity, and therefore two-way collaboration with anyone, including suppliers, will sit here as an uneasy concept.

This involves the way people choose to manage and clearly the method used is a choice, albeit for some people, an unconscious and therefore unconsidered one.

159

# Styles of Managing

As individuals, people will have their own style and in the modern organisational process there are varied styles found. For the sake of simplicity, we have used the word 'leaders' below, rather than procurement managers, or supply relationship managers etc.

When the leaders apply a particular style, this personal style will then automatically become an example to others. It can represent an input into people and can therefore determine the outcomes that the leader has created consciously or unconsciously.

The particular style being used by leaders will, therefore, have a dramatic effect on an organisation. It seems logical to ensure the intended result will follow from an intended style input.

Views on leader and manager styles follow: these are "extremes"/polarised views to highlight and compare/contrast the differences:

1) A command and control style: the "older" and militaristic way:
- keeps control
- people are "held onto"
- judgmental
- "tells"
- see though a "pinhole"
- directive
- "push" approach

2) A coaching style: the "newer" and empowering way:
- lets people try
- people are given a "self release"
- non-judgmental
- "sells"
- sees the wider view
- supportive
- "pull" approach

3) Autocratic and aggressive people:
- drive and push people and are not leaders
- has a "single", "my" viewpoint
- one way communicator
- demanding "do it my way, now"
- takes "fixed my way positions" and engages in a contest of will
- makes threats and applies pressure
- engenders a blame and fear culture where people are fearful of trying something new, and remain within the status quo and "doing it by the book"
- people will cover up genuine mistakes and therefore will stifle the learning opportunity that was presented

4) Procrastinator and passive people:
- abdicate from taking decisions
- use group viewpoints
- indecisive but they believe there are being democratic
- "what do you all want to do, whenever"
- changes positions easily and avoids any contest
- makes offers and yields to pressure
- engenders a lazy and stagnant culture where people eventually will increasingly become less interested and frustrated by the lack of action and direction; the good people will move on, the not so good people will stay

5) Charismatic and assertive people:
- pulls more than pushes
- two-way communicator
- people follow naturally, is a leader
- makes concessions, "I think this, what do we think?"
- problem solves and explores interests
- partnership views and reasons
- looks for objective criteria and yields to principles not pressure
- engenders a progressive culture where people become committed and supportive to each other; team work will flourish easily

Style is also largely a matter of personal choice. Leaders therefore have an enormous responsibility to ensure an appropriate "sowing" style is undertaken so that the eventual "reaping" is the planned, what was desired, outcome.

It seems irrefutable, from the above extreme views, which two styles will be the most effective in most circumstances in most organisations. Those that noted (2) and (5) are correct! This is not to say that the other styles have no part to play. For example the directive commander and the autocrat maybe needed when dealing with procrastinators and when dealing with emergencies.

It is also interesting to speculate which styles get the best responses and which ones suit more effective supplier relationships.

As we have seen earlier, power plays from buying only possibly have any part to play in leverage items and even then, this should mean not using that power to "close down" suppliers. One of the disadvantages however with tendering on leverage items, is that the suppliers regularly get no constructive feedback if they are unsuccessful. Over time they may choose to no longer tender. However, when using reverse e-auctions for leverage items, suppliers should then have visibility of the award price; positive feedback indeed.

Additionally power plays may also have unethical effects and it was reported in *Supply Management 24 April 2008* from a poll of 100 buyers that 20% of buyers have been offered bribes by suppliers.

Headlines in *The Sunday Times* of 16 March 2008 were *"Sainsbury's in £3 million scandal over potato bungs"* and continued *"...we are the victims of an alleged crime and take it very seriously. None of the payments went through our system and we believe this was limited to one supplier."*

Bribery takes "two to tango" and suppliers are, of course, not blameless here and may be balancing the risk of losing business against the cost of, and any comeback from, offering bribes.

## Buying and collaboration

As seen earlier in the discussion on power in part 2.0, the buyer's behaviour, linked to Kraljic, may be as follows:

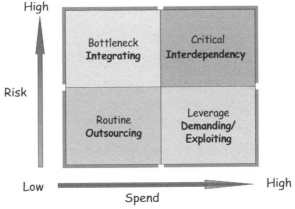

In turn, the link to more collaborative approaches may be seen as follows:

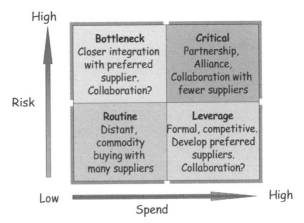

Recall, however, that relationships between suppliers and buyers may also involve an uneven distribution of power, especially in the buying process.

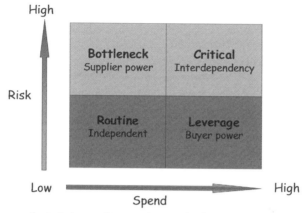

This readily illustrates the imbalance of power that can be found:
*   Leverage buying is where there are many suppliers with a buyer buying large quantities and the buyer is therefore able to leverage on price.
*   Bottleneck items are where there are few suppliers but the buyer has to have their highly priced products; for example, OEM spares and inkjet printer cartridges.

In turn, related to risks, then we can see a strategic and tactical approach to procurement forming, as follows:

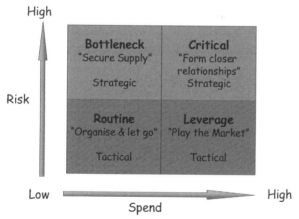

We can also see there are variations in relationships, and six types may be identified below, ranging from tactical leverage buying to strategic alliance relationships, like for example, found with Toyota car assembly in the UK where key suppliers actually sit on the Toyota management board.

There are also varied levels of trust, openness and information exchange that results in varied types of relationships involved:

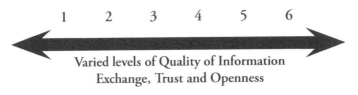

**Varied levels of Quality of Information Exchange, Trust and Openness**

| **Tactical** | **Strategic** |
|---|---|
| Distant | Closer |
| "Deal for me" | "In it together" |
| Shorter Term | Longer Term |
| Level 1 Trust (Contractual) | Level 3 Trust (Goodwill) |

We can expand this further where:

**Tactical procurement** uses the new trainee and junior buyers, and has the following types of relationships:

1. Adversary relationships; "Take it or leave it".
2. Transactional relationships; Normal ordering.
3. Single Source relationships; Exclusive agreements usually at fixed price for a specific time.

**Strategic procurement** uses the more senior buyers with the following types of relationships:

4. Strategic alliance relationships; Working together for a specific purpose.
5. Collaborative relationships; Commitment with shared risks/benefits.
6. Co-destiny relationships; Interdependency.

Relating this back to Kraljic, the following gives us an ideal-typical perspective:

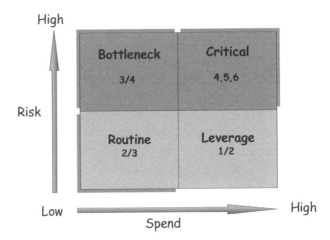

Keeping our ideal-typical view, we can note the following stereotypes on transactional and collaborative approaches.

**Transactional relationships** have the following characteristics:

- Short term
- Separated/arms length
- Wiifm (what's in it for me)
- "One-off"
- Low contact/closed
- Little trust
- Price dominates
- "One night stand"
- Power based
- Win/lose
- One way (customer demands sensitive data)
- Customer keeps all cost savings
- All risk with supplier, customer risks zero
- Power based "spin"
- Adversarial and inefficient
- Hierarchical /superior subordinate
- Blame culture
- High formal controls
- Rigid contracts
- Alienated employees
- Predatory
- Technical Performance specifications "rule"

Whereas **Collaborative relationships** are typified by the following:

- Long term
- Close/alliance
- Wiifu (what's in it for us)
- "Forever"
- Shared vision/open
- Trust/risk/benefits
- Shared destiny
- "Marriage"
- Equality based
- Win/win
- Two-way exchange of sensitive data
- Mutual to reduce costs, times and waste
- Shared risk and benefits
- Pragmatic trust
- Challenging to implement and continue with
- Equality

- Problem solving culture
- Self controlled
- Flexible contracts
- Motivated employees
- Proactive
- Work beyond just "one" technical view

**Changing the thinking**

To move to be more strategic or to change the way we manage relationships, there is a need to change the thinking. Some important points on our thinking are as follows:

- Our thinking comes from our mental maps.
- These are like computer programmes that give predetermined actions.
- For example, the attitudes /beliefs /values, that gives us our "reality."
- With computer programmes we will check and re-calibrate the parameters when needed, for example, with independent/random demand.
- But, how often do we challenge our own mental map parameters?
- Changing our thinking means acquiring different perspectives, but such change may be uncomfortable and may be rejected, for example: "Trust is the emotional glue that involves commitment to others" versus "Emotions have no part to play in business".

**How do we think?**

The simplified view is as follows:

- Logical left brain: Rational facts-based reasoning that converges.
- Creative right brain: Emotional "feelings" synthesis that diverges.

Meanwhile, "rounded people" can use both sides.

Our thinking works through into company thinking and how we manage the supply chain. Our book *"The Relationship driven Supply Chain; creating a culture of collaboration throughout the chain" (2006)*, explores this type of thinking further with some suggestions about the need to change from linear/in box thinking to more systems based/network thinking.
As noted there: *"Thinking differently and looking for more creative and innovative ways to manage the supply chain may be a future only a few organisations are able to undertake".*

# Relationships are central to business success

In this regard, it needs to be appreciated, that changing to more relationship ways of managing suppliers can mean that the current people may not the best ones to do this and if this means changing the current buyers, then so be it, as relationship based approaches may be a new skill set that some current staff are unable to develop.

What has to be fundamental is the belief that relationships must be handled, with all of the internal and external supply-chain players. Indeed, improving relationships is one of the main keys to enable procurement, supply chain and business success.

Relationship management must be a company strategy, and become a core capability within the company, especially also as there are costs associated with poor business relationships, including:

- High administration costs.
- Time spend price wrangling.
- Time spent resolving problems.
- Too many meetings with too many people.
- Unwilling to consider simple solutions to problems.
- An atmosphere that discourages innovation.

Toyota in *Institute of Business Ethics, Supplier Relationships report 2006*

### Change at the interfaces

There is clearly plenty of evidence to suggest that any power-based transactional approach is not the best "one stop shop" strategy.

The supply chain is a series of joined dependencies with variability's and interfaces, and, as we have observed in Emmett and Crocker 2006: *"Managing a dependent process in isolation and managing it independently is plain folly. Managing the supply chain without the collaboration of the other players is a fruitless strategy."*

This will need collaboration at the interfaces between people within and between organisations and will involve the following:

- Selective dialogue between the "right" people in suppliers and customers.
- Intense and focused activity involving investments of time/resources from the all of the organisations involved.
- Taking the long term and strategic view so as to improve the performance of the whole supply chain.

Collaboration is not any of the following:

- A software package.
- "I will take all the benefits".
- A quick fix.
- Easy.
- For everyone.
- A "one size fits all" approach.

### Lessons from Experience on Relationships

- *"We have to be interested in being criticised"* .
- *"Business is increasingly interdependent, where action takes place between and not within"* .
- *"Trying to get through years of accumulated baggage is tough"*.
- *"Personal relationships that bridge former gaps in communications between vendor and retailer are what can really spell success"*.

**Collaboration works**
At the construction of T5 London Heathrow Airport, besides the buyer/supplier pre-requisites of trust and the cost sharing of any savings or overruns, there were many collaborative aspects involved in the T5 contract, as follows:

## The T5 Contract

The T5 Agreement is central to everything that's good about Terminal 5. It is BAA's response to a project whose sheer size and complexity defy traditional construction management techniques. Legally-binding, in essence it's a contract in reverse. Instead of specifying what redress can be taken in the event of things going wrong, it aims to stop problems happening in the first place. This is done by fostering constructive behaviour and a recrimination-free environment.

### Key features include:
*Ownership of risk*
In contrast to most so-called partnership deals, risk is not shared between client and contractors. BAA carries it all, allowing contractors to concentrate on delivering results. The focus is on managing out the cause of problems, not their effects if they do happen.

*Complexity management*
The task of building T5 is split into 16 main projects, plus 147 sub-projects of between £30 million and £150 million each. The agreement binds BAA and its 60 key first-tier' suppliers only, these suppliers are themselves responsible for the appointment and management of second- and third-tier suppliers, who must also work within the spirit of the agreement.

*Close supplier involvement*
To avoid the traditional and potentially damaging demarcation between design and build, key suppliers were brought on board at a much earlier stage in the planning process than is usual. This enabled potential hitches to be spotted before designs were finalised and construction began.

*Integrated teamwork*
Both within and across teams, the concentration has been on proactive problem-solving rather than the avoidance of litigation.

*Shared values*
Common induction programmes and regular communication initiatives help to ensure that all of the 6,000 workers from 400 supplier organisations who can be involved at any given time share the same values and objectives, which include being proud of working on T5 and delivering the project on time, on budget, to quality and safely.

**Human Resources November 2004.**

168

Clearly T5 represents more than just a cost-plus contract, but also a whole different collaborative relationship with suppliers.

# Making the change

What, fundamentally, will have to change when following a collaborative approach? Well, this topic has been more fully covered in *"The Relationship Driven Supply Chain" (2006)* by Emmett and Crocker, but to note here: people first, and also the following:

- Contracts to simple flexible approaches.
- Intensive management involvement.
- Periodic performance monitoring.
- Internal controls for confidential information.
- Problem solving procedures.
- Supplier is seen as a customer = "reverse customer service" or "supplier service" (referred to earlier) as what suppliers do affects what happens to the customer.
- Cross-functional supplier/customer teams.
- Hub (supply chain managers) and spoke (suppliers/customer) organisations? And people...as "people change one at a time".

It is people that change a company, and it is the people who make the relationships in, and between, organisations. The changing of company culture ("what is down around here") will need to pass through the following stages:

| Aspect | "Stormy/Blame" Culture | "Steady/Sane" Culture | "Sunny/Gain" Culture |
|---|---|---|---|
| Goals | Announced | Communicated | Agreed |
| Information | Status symbol and power based | Traded | Abundant |
| Motivation | Manipulative | Focused on staff needs | A clear goal |
| Decisions | From above | Partly delegated | Staff take them |
| Mistakes | Are only made by staff | Responsibility is taken | Are allowed as learning lessons |
| Conflicts | Are unwelcome and "put down" | Are mastered | Source of new innovation |
| Control | From above | Partly delegated | Fully delegated |
| Management Style | Authoritarian/ aggressive | Cooperative | Participative/ Assertive |
| Authority | Requires obedience | Requires cooperation | Requires collaboration |
| Manager | Absolute ruler and feels superior | Problem solver and decision maker | Change strategist and self confident |

Once the culture has been defined, this will need the examination of all internal and external relationships. Trust will often remain a major barrier; however, without trust, there will be no relationship.

## Managing Change

To move forward and make changes to the way we operate both as an individual and as a business may not be easy. Many also seem to forget that changing organisations involves changing people, and this includes themselves. As observed by Ghandi: *"Be the change you want to see in the world."*

Change is the one constant of life. The only certain aspect of the future is that it will be different; a future of stable turbulence. It is in the dealing with this uncertainty in the future that managing change becomes a key business function.

## Sources of change

Most people will have noticed the following trends and resulting changes in recent times:

| From Old Ways | Towards New Ways |
| --- | --- |
| Technology/product / supply | Customer/Market/Demand |
| "Push" product flows | "Pull " product flows |
| Product Sells | Customer Buys |
| Manage People | Manage Messages |
| Specialist Skills | Broad Skills |
| Bureaucratic control | Empowerment |
| Instruction/telling | Consulting/Selling |
| Job for life | Portfolio jobs |
| Earning a living | Learning a living |
| Adversarial | Partnership |
| Fire-fighting | Fire-lighting |

## Reactions to change

Change can be dramatic and can, if handled wrongly, be traumatic, as changes will always impact on people. The impact will vary and whilst all the people involved will experience the same steps when facing change, the impacts are likely to be at different times. People find their own time to go through change; people change one at a time and not usually all at the same time.

The following table shows the steps that are involved, along with some typical responses. Step one will commence when a person first hears about the change.

| Step of change | Comments | "Here" to "there" |
| --- | --- | --- |
| 1. Shock, immobilised | "They can not do it" | Past orientation |
| 2. Denial | "We will never do it" | Past |
| 3. Frustration and defensive | "It is just too difficult" | Past |
| 4. Acceptance and discarding | "I might try" | Past/ Future |
| 5. Testing | "Lets try" | Future |
| 6. Search for meaning | "It seems to work" | Future |
| 7. Integration | "I can do it" | Future |

Change will often, therefore, be resisted, because it can mean "changing the way things have always been done around here".

People's attitudes to change will vary in any group of individual people. These attitudes can be very emotional and wide ranging, for example:

- Stimulating to Resisting.
- Exciting to Denying.
- Pleasure to Fear.
- Anticipation to Anger.
- Enthusiastic to Stress.

- Exciting to Concern.
- Challenging to Worrying.
- Opportunity to Certainty.
- Visionary and looking forward to staying with the current situation.

It is critical to appreciate that all people will go through such emotional responses, but they will do it differently and at different times. Leaders and managers need to be alert to such variations and to manage them effectively. After all, people have to change one at a time.

Resistance to change can however be minimised when the change aligns with the following:

- Is agreed by all.
- Is owned by individuals.
- Is supported by leadership and management.
- Follows the culture and values.
- Decreases current problems.
- Increases new experiences and interests.
- Emotions are understood by management.
- Reactions are allowed to be discussed with management.
- Does not cause a persons personal security to be threatened.

**Change and communication**

Managing change is a skilful process, and a key skill is communication. It has been said that communication and change are synonymous, as people can be "in fear", uncertain, and therefore need to be clearly communicated with. It is critical to involve people, communicate, listen, give people chance to air objections, and to give people time to adapt. This should involve making the following choices in the methods of communication:

- Not "telling" propaganda, but "selling" proper communication.
- Inform people at all stages.
- Ask them questions to uncover feeling.
- Listen carefully to the answers.
- Use written communications only where they are appropriate.
- Concentrate mainly, on face to face communication, as these provide for more effective communication (as we shall see shortly).
- Consult wherever possible.
- Admit any mistakes and learn from them.
- Celebrate individuals and group success.
- Be as open as you can be.

Communication will need to have the following keys:

- "The objective of communication is to prevent misunderstanding".
- "It is NOT a one-off exercise but is continual, and needed over and over again".
- In change it needs to be: "Communicate - communicate - communicate".

**Change Principles for People**

1. Honesty - so that people can trust.
2. Aims - so that people can participate in a clear sense of mission or purpose - the simpler the better.
3. Uncertainty is unsettling.
4. Participation gives a commitment for results. Getting involved works.
5. Recognition of people's effort scores higher, than material rewards.
6. Mature individuality is needed - traditional cultures often do not like this - but they also expect people to behave like adults!
7. Full commitment of all those affected or involved with the change.
8. Clearly linked values with behaviour promote trust.
9. Team working and good inter-personal relationships.
10. A shared vision and a defined role in that vision.
11. Time is needed to maintain quality.
12. Individual's attitudes and behaviour will have to change.
13. Team involvement and approaches work.
14. People make changes happen therefore, emotional needs are involved.
15. Takes time and quick fixes will usually fail.
16. Plans are needed to serve and not to enslave.
17. Plan in short intervals with flexible priorities. Be the tortoise and not the hare.
18. Performance at the start will suffer before the improvement works through.
19. Find people throughout the organisation, who are interested and have relevant skills/ high energy levels, and use them as change champions wherever they are in the organisation.
20. There is a risk that taking time can appear to be indecisive. Therefore, a person losing their motivation is a risk.

**Force Fields in Change**

There are always people who are against change and also those who are for the change; the so-called blockers and backers. These must be identified as far as possible so that we have a good and realistic view of the stakeholders, sponsors and end-users. The following will need to be considered:

- Gather as much information as possible on the wants and concerns of the sponsors and the end-users of the change.
- Who authorises and agrees (the deciders)?
- Who wants change and needs convincing (the friends who will recommend)?
- Who does not want change (the enemies)?
- Who implements and influences the recommenders?
- Who are the experts/ people listened to (by the deciders)?
- Who limits access to the deciders (gatekeepers)?

Next, an attempt can be made to resolve, by weighting, the forces favouring and resisting the change and listing the pros and the cons. The following example shows this where the longer the arrow, then the greater is the influence it exerts and also in which direction. Is the force stronger?

| Forces for | Forces Against |
|---|---|
| Recognize that need to change → | ← Loss of security |
| Pressure from users → | ← Fear of unknown |
| Poor performance ⟶ | ←Tradition |
| Work backlogs → | ← Agreed working practices |
| Competition → | ← Loss of productivity |
| Management wants it → | ←Threats to status |

# Project Management

Project management has some useful planning and controlling techniques and viewpoints. If, therefore, we recognise that making changes to Supplier Management practices involve us in the reality of managing a change project, then beside the change aspects discussed above, the following project aspects can also be usefully considered. The application of many of these aspects will also be seen, later, in Part 6.0.

### Fundamental Questions
*   What is the ultimate objective we are trying to achieve?
*   What means (tools, people, and methods) is available?
*   What are the requirements?
*   How can success be measured?
*   What is the timeline?
*   What is the budget?
*   How will we organise the project?
*   How do we intend to inform and communicate?

# Project leader

Someone will need to lead the initiative and to follow the following guidelines:
*   Ensure that there is a Sponsor at high level in the organisation who overtly demonstrates their commitment to the project.
*   Plan, plan, plan. Do not be too eager to initially handle the more interesting aspects without having a sufficiently detailed plan that is signed off by all key stakeholders
*   Ensure that the various roles and responsibilities are clearly defined, accepted and understood by all key stakeholders.
*   Identify and constantly re-visit the critical success factors and change project risks - focus on results.
*   Have "go/no-go" decision points at key milestones on the change project plan.
*   Constantly monitor compliance with the intended scope to try and prevent over-runs as far as possible.
*   Do not cut corners to meet any unrealistic deadlines. If this has to be done for business reasons, ensure that the Sponsor understands the consequences and demonstrates full ownership.

- Ensure key stakeholders expectations are managed throughout the change project.
- Build team spirit, momentum and motivation. Get over any of the temporary failures and always celebrate successes.
- Learn from your change project. Conduct a project post-mortem or benefits realisation exercise that identifies the project's strengths and weaknesses.

The project leader will need to ask themselves the following questions:

- What knowledge and skills do you have?
- What have you learnt from previous change projects?
- Will you be on secondment?
- Are you expected to do two full-time jobs?
- What do you want to get out of the change project?
- Who will carry out your appraisal?
- What is the communication with your line boss?
- Who cares for the needs of fellow project workers?
- Who does your solution need to perform for?
- What benefits should be produced?
- What costs/penalties are to be avoided?
- What limitations/restrictions apply?
- What do you what to happen?
- What do you not want to happen?

# SWOT and Risk Analysis

At the start it is useful to conduct a SWOT (Strengths/Weaknesses, Opportunities/Threats) analysis to determine how things are now and where they want to be at the end of the project. This SWOT analysis can ask the following two sets of questions:

1. *List the Internal Strengths/Weaknesses*
- People /management expertise.
- Facilities/building and equipment.
- Technology.
- Marketing and sales skills.
- Reputation and image.
- Financial resources.

2. *List the External Opportunities/Threats*
   These are the "what ifs" that could prevent the change project failing:
- Political, social, economic changes.
- Competition, locally or globally.
- Market size and trends.
- Profitability.
- Needs that products/services fulfil.
- Likelihood of changes to any of these.

174

It will also assist the process if the risks involved are assessed, and the following may be used:

- Brainstorm with the team the direct and indirect risks.
- For each risk identified, indicate the likelihood of it materialising on a three point scale: very likely/possible/not very likely.
- For each risk, indicate the impact of it materialising on a three point scale: high/medium/low.
- Prioritise the risks from the likelihood (step 2: most likely/possible/ not very likely) and prioritise from the impacts (step 3: high /medium/ low).
- For each risk, determine the controls steps that need to be implemented to manage the risk.
- Get the sponsor to sign off the risk management plan.

# Continuous improvement and Kaizen

Effective SRM attempts to nurture a culture of continuous improvement/Kaizen from key trading partners. Therefore this section will provide a brief summary of how Kaizen operates and how it can assist in developing supplier's performance.

Kaizen is a word meaning "continuous improvement" and comes from two Japanese words: Kai meaning transforming and Zen, meaning worth/value.

Everyone is encouraged to come up with small improvement suggestions on a regular basis. This is not a once-a-month or once-a-year activity. It is continuous, and in Japanese organisations, such as Toyota and Canon, a total of 60 to 70 suggestions per employee per year are written down, shared and implemented.

In most cases, these are not ideas for major changes. Kaizen is based on making little changes on a regular basis: always improving productivity, safety and effectiveness whilst reducing waste. The Kaizen philosophy is to "do it better, make it better and improve it even if it isn't broken, because if we don't, we can't compete with those who do."

In supply chains, Kaizen encompasses many of the components of Japanese organisations that have been seen as a part of their success. Quality circles, automation, suggestion systems, just-in-time delivery and Kanban are all included within the Kaizen system of running a business. Kaizen involves setting standards and then continually improving those standards. To support the higher standards Kaizen also involves providing the training, materials and supervision that is needed for suppliers to achieve the higher standards and maintain their ability to meet those standards on an on-going basis.

### Kaizen and SRM

In terms of supplier relationship management, it must be remembered, as we saw earlier with the Relationship Positioning Tool (RPT) that it is the approach, actions and attitudes of both sides of the contractual relationship, which must change in order that there is a culture of continuous improvement.

## Case Study: BMW

BMW are continually consulting with their key suppliers in an effort to reduce costs by four billion over a four-year period.

Teams of Procurement, Logistics and Quality experts consult with suppliers during workshops to evaluate areas of improvement. BMW believe that large cost reductions can be made throughout the supply chain.

By encouraging improved efficiency and effectiveness throughout the supply chain, BMW hope to continually improve workflows and significantly reduce supplier lead-times.

The following outlines some of the key philosophies of a Kaizen approach.
- The consequences of change cannot be predicted = We are all learning together; we being our company and our suppliers.
- Without shared vision there can be no shared goals = Sharing our objectives with our suppliers.
- Vision is constant = Mutual objectives and goals, are developed, which are continually shared with the suppliers.
- Alignment can only be achieved through empowerment = Empowering our suppliers.

## Case Study: Dairy Crest

Dairy Crest have introduced three key targets for Procurement:

- Greater Supplier Innovation
- Increasing the influence of Procurement over the total spend
- Improving Supplier relationships

Their approach is centred on procurement unlocking expertise, both within their company and within their suppliers. Their overall spend of £400 million is expected to reduce as they look to the supply chain to encourage innovation.

An increased focus on supplier relationships will seek to improve sustainable procurement.

Continuous Improvement, or Kaizen, involves the improvement of all aspects of an organisation's interfaces with suppliers. Suppliers are an asset, and innovative suppliers are potentially very valuable in value-added terms. The authors have experience of procurement functions that have actually been seen as blockers when it comes to harnessing innovation.

If procurement departments wish to continue to grow their influence, they have to be more forward-looking and open-minded in terms of driving innovation. It is not just the coming up with new ideas which is important, but also being the facilitator for channelling alternative ideas from the supply chain. This not only requires more internal collaboration, but also improved supply chain relationships. Small continuous changes, like the following, are easier to make and less daunting than single major improvements.

- Puts the "customer" and" supplier" at the forefront of the organisations activities.
- Identifies both the "internal" and "external" customers of the organisation.
- Aims at constant improvements.
- Involves a cross-functional approach.
- Utilises techniques such as the tools of TQM/5Ss/6 Sigma.
- Emphasises early involvement and empowerment of suppliers.

The Procurement department contribution involves improvements in all aspects of its activities:

- Relationships with other internal departments and service to them.
- Improved service to suppliers.
- Improved quality of supplies.
- Improved service from suppliers.
- Improvements in systems.
- Improved operating procedures.

It is people at all levels who are responsible for suggesting and introducing these improvements.

## Case Study: Ford

To the Ford Motor Company, continuous supplier improvement means that internal and external suppliers strive to achieve the following goals:

- Understand and improve organisational systems and processes
- Use statistical process control in measuring performance of quality criteria
- Establish targets for significant process and product characteristics and reduce variation around these targets
- Obtain timely internal and external customer feedback data
- Establish a rating system and measure customer perceptions of products and services
- Identify principal and best-in-class competition to assess the quality of processes, products and services
- Develop a cost of quality system
- Educate employees in quality
- Assist customers and suppliers, as partners, to improve the quality of their products and services

# Case Study: Dunlop Cox

In the automotive industry, vehicle manufacturers are increasingly unwilling to pay their component suppliers more their products. In other words, higher costs of wages or of materials for example, cannot be recouped from price increases. This concept of no price increases operates widely in the Japanese manufacturing industry.

As many world-class Japanese manufacturers, including the car makers Honda, Nissan and Toyota, have invested in the UK, the approach has gathered pace. Suppliers to these Japanese organisations and other car makers must improve their efficiency if their profit margins are to be maintained. In most organisations this will involve continuous improvement.

## Small but Continuous Improvements

The Japanese have demonstrated that to be more efficient, organisations to not necessarily have to follow the capital investment route. The Japanese way is to go for small but continuous improvements of a fraction of a percent initiated by the people on the shop floor. It is a much safer alternative and the Japanese are the world's leading practitioners of continuous improvement or, as they call it, Kaizen.

At Dunlop Cox, which makes seat slides, frames and mechanisms for customers such as Nissan, Rolls Royce, Rover, Saab and Volvo, a continuous improvement programme was introduced. It followed the introduction of Cellular and Just-In-Time (JIT) manufacture. The company believed then, as now, that if other manufacturers had benefited from Kaizen, it would too.

Like most manufacturers, it had an intelligent workforce with a detailed knowledge of the production process. If those people could be persuaded to contribute ideas and suggestions for improvement – for eliminating waste – the process could begin.

The teams collect ideas, discuss what is to be done, implement it and every two months report to the directors. The directors' job is to disseminate good ideas across the company, not to interfere with the improvement process. Some of the results used the Japanese maxims that if it costs a lot of money, don't do it. For example, for an outlay of $11,000 in one cell, a saving of $200,000 (or 13 jobs) was achieved. The new cell layout used less space. Product flow was better, work-in-progress was reduced and quality was increased.

## Benefits of Kaizen

Kaizen clearly has many benefits. It does not cost much money. The productivity gains are high and they are being delivered by many people, not just by production management.

There is no resistance to Kaizen because the ideas for improvement are initiated on the shop floor and carried out there.

Shop floor involvement in Kaizen, which should be voluntary not compulsory, creates a better atmosphere in the factory.

External relationships with customers also improve. They have less to complain about because a knock on effect of increased productivity is increased reliability of the product and its delivery.

# Part five: Summary

- SRM requires a 2 way transparent information exchange.
- Information sharing starts internally.
- Suppler development has a positive impact on quality and financial performance.
- There are many options available to develop suppliers.
- Improving supplier relationships minimises supply risk.
- Supplier management is assisted by electronic management systems and collaboration.
- Collaboration requires trust and soft skills development.
- Supply chain management supports supplier management as working with supplier gives benefits for all parties, however Buyers behaviour may have to change.
- Managing change, however, is a constant in the 21st century; therefore, techniques of managing change, project management and continuous improvement/Kaizen are useful to facilitate supplier development implementation.

# Part six: Conclusion

## The role of Procurement

In this regard, we will start with a summary of what we said at the start of this book:

- Procurement must recognise that suppliers are critically important in the provision of new ideas, innovation and value that can increase the performance of the organisation.
- Procurement should share a joint common agenda with suppliers to meet customer requirements. Procurement will recognise that its own organisations performance is indelibly connected to the performance of its suppliers.
- Procurement will be committed to its key suppliers for mutual benefit and gain over the medium- to long-term, and will work together for continuous improvements year on year by having a joint restless search for inter-linked improvements.
- Procurement will ensure that "fit for purpose," supplier selection and evaluation is undertaken, and that this key activity is not rule-bound or covered by restrictive bureaucratic procedures that are now out of date.
- Procurement will recognise that the supply chain is a series of internal and external cross-functional processes and procurement will be an active and willing and leading member of the internal cross functional structure that connects to all of the external supply processes.

Unfortunately, we are both of the opinion that many organisations often fail or perhaps, stumble, in managing their suppliers. We have shown in the text that this is because the internal customer, or worse, someone else, is left to manage the selected suppliers, without perhaps realising that they have to!

Whilst the internal customer will often provide the kickstart to a procurement department (with the need and the specification), who then takes this over by sourcing a supplier and the eventual placing of the order/contract?

After this, procurement departments so often "wave the order goodbye" and the internal customer is left without having any conscious commitment to continue the procurement process cycle. This is sub-optimal; a classic example of a cross-functional, dependent process failing at the interfaces between departments.

There is, often, little understanding of just how a procurement department relates to, or gets involved with the essential supplier management in the procurement process. Whilst some departments are able to do this, other departments will just oversee the supplier management, whilst there are even some procurement departments that will ignore it completely.

This book, therefore, has concentrated on highlighting the need for better supplier management, improving supplier management and gives guidelines on how to better manage contracts and develop suppliers. The organisational responsibly for this is routed

180

and determined by an organisation's specific structure, which in turn, is a policy matter for the strategic leaders of an individual organisations. It cannot be systematically expected that supplier management is *automatically* going to be a procurement department role, as there is just no "one size fits all model" for organisational structure.

We have tried to answer the question "What kind of relationship do I need with suppliers so I can get the best from them, and therefore the best for me?" In order to amplify this further, we have presented, below, some applied aspects of contract management by looking at one specific application which has some wider applications.

# Managing 3PL (third party logistics) Contractors

This case study looks specifically at the outsourcing and subsequent management of the selected logistics (transport/warehousing) contractors. Whilst this is a service, it also has good indicators for managing large-scale contracts, such as construction, the supply of goods etc. Indeed, when reading this section, substituting the "3PL" context for other suppliers/ contractors is a valuable learning exercise.

It can be seen that any contract management activities will always cover three areas:

1. Contract administration; handles the formal governance of the contract and changes to the contract documentation.
2. Commercial and service delivery management; ensures that the service is being delivered as agreed, to the required level of performance and quality.
3. Collaboration and relationship management; keeps the relationship between the two parties open and constructive, aiming to resolve or ease tensions and identify problems early.
   **After:** Office of Government Commerce 2002 Contract Management Guidelines-principles for service contracts.

All of the above activities have to be managed, with the third one, especially, being poorly handled by many organisations. This is important to appreciate, as managing suppliers and contracts it is more than mere governance and ensuring "they" do what the contract says. The "added extra" comes from being proactive in the relationship area. This is especially so in long-term contracts, where interdependency between customer and provider is inevitable, and it is, therefore, in the interests of all parties to make the relationship work.

Factors for success in relationships have been extensively covered in this book; briefly, these factors are trust/respect, communication and recognition of mutual aims. All of these factors are well understood by Toyota as shown in the following 3PL case study, where it will be seen they have some excellent supplier management methods which focus (in our view, correctly) on the relationship aspects:

# Case Study: Toyota USA & Freight Provider Selection

Toyota-NAPO (North American Parts Operation) is responsible for receiving and shipping $2 billion worth of service parts and accessories globally. The Toyota Way can be called a mindset and an attitude. Toyota says, "It is the way we approach our work and our relationships with others". The Toyota Way is based upon two pillars:
* Continuous Improvement
* Respect for People

Each pillar has five (5) major principals:
- Challenge
- Kaizen
- Genchi Genbutsu (Go look, go see)
- Teamwork
- Respect

**NAPO Mission Statement**
*"To provide our customers with the right parts at the right time in the right place at the lowest cost", Toyota felt compelled to translate this message into one that would be applicable to their carriers. The translation would allow them to effectively convey the right message to their carrier partners, thereby connecting all of the parties, at least, philosophically.*

*"At NAPO, we wanted our mission statement to convey the following: the Toyota philosophy; the objectives that NAPO strives to achieve; and to lay the foundation for the expectations that will be placed on the carriers".*

**Carrier Relationships with Toyota**
Relationships are based on three (3) principals:
* Mutual Trust
* Respect
* Work together to reduce waste

Toyota only seeks new carriers when:
* A new facility or new geographical responsibility is required
* A new program such as returnable program is required
* The existing Carrier is closing down
* The business objectives change and a carrier is unable to accommodate new requirements
* Carrier is no longer able to do an effective job and countermeasures have not been successful

When looking for replacements, the NAPO bid process is initially issued only to those carriers who are current partners, or, if the transportation requires a niche or specialized carrier, then they may bid the business to new carriers.

**How Does NAPO Select New Carriers?**
By incorporating all of the principals addressed above, Toyota's selection criteria are presented in a manner that tests the viability of their philosophy and principals:
- Can the partners build a successful relationship?
- Will the Toyota Way be realized?
- Will the partnership withstand the long term, 5, 10, or 15 years?
- What are the business drivers?
- What is the legislative environment?
- What issues or challenges may be on the horizon?

**What does it mean to be a Toyota NAPO Carrier?**
Toyota has established a set of guidelines that will help the partnership prosper. Through this process the parties reaffirm their principles by employing the following techniques:

- Continuously seek improvement
  - Can we move this part better?
  - Faster?
  - Cheaper?
  - Most importantly: All three constraints are balanced equally.
- Toyota will not compromise:
  - We will not give up quality to save a buck
  - Do not carry more inventory if it does not make financial sense
- Genchi Genbutsu
  - Who better to tell how we can improve than those actually doing the work! Ask your partners, what can we do to be a better shipper? And listen!
- Teamwork
  - We took for "partners" to achieve Respect, not "vendors & carriers"

Toyota-NAPO has established and maintains a process that defines the organisation and its philosophy in ways that foster the development of strong logistics partnerships.

**www.transportgistics.com**

Clearly, here, the relationship aspects are given a high level of importance and represent the main key aspects of the "deal" for 3PL service suppliers. These methods are also in line with the following general product and materials supply practices in Japan:

# Checklist: Supplies Practices in Japan

### General
- Suppliers are given clear specifications and blanket orders
- Predictable supply schedules

- Fewer and local suppliers
- Long-term "for life" intention
- Joint investigation of problems
- Joint improvement and innovation
- Quality circles team approach

**Requirements**
- Zero defects
- Frequent JIT deliveries of small batches
- Short supply lead-times

**Effects**
- Quick process changeovers
- Elimination of inspection on receipt
- Zero defects production and logistics
- Total quality control
- High quality at lower cost and increased productivity
- Early identification of scrap and defects
- Low inventory carry costs
- Released cash
- Minimum paperwork controls
- Fast response to customers requirements

**Defining 3PL**
Typical logistics services considered for outsourcing to a third party include the following:

- Warehousing (facilities, MHE, racking, labour).
- Transport (inbound/outbound).
- Freight Consolidation/Distribution/Cross-Docking.
- Product Labelling/Packaging.
- Product Returns and Repairs.
- Stock reporting.

When any one of these services is transferred from in-house service to a separate logistics provider via an agreement for a specified period of time, then outsourcing has occurred, and a logistics contract with a third party is established. However, the contract has to live, and this is why and where the relationship aspects do become critical. As explained earlier in the book, resorting to or threatening the use of legal contractual aspects should not be the initial preferred action when things do not happen as expected.

**Outsourcing**
Outsourcing can have a profound impact on an organisations financial performance; therefore there are a number of issues to be considered before making the decision. The first is whether logistics is a core competency. If this is critical to an organisation, like warehousing is for

Amazon, then it may be this is central to the organisations strategy, and, therefore, a decision is made to maintain all, or part, of the current in-house operations.

The second main reason is financial, and whilst logistics service providers may argue that they can lower costs, this may not apply where organisations are already running an efficient operation. If an organisations competition is outsourcing, there then may be an opportunity to use a 3PL with experience in your operations, which may allow some leverage of this experience, for example, opportunities to consolidate similar consignments to get full truckloads from less-than-full truckloads, as such synergies cannot be done internally.

Other financial reasons relate to the fact that, as logistics is a low margin business, your own people and resources can be better employed on more profitable work, or the limited available capital is now invested in an area that give deliver a better return; e.g. retailers using capital to open more shops/outlets. Without a mandate from top management, outsourcing will fail. Additionally the organisation must have people with the skills to manage an outsourced relationship. Those skills are very different from managing transport/warehouse operations, for example, good warehouse managers are not necessarily going to any good at managing 3PL relationships.

The final question a company should ask is whether it is outsourcing for the right reasons. Too often, companies outsource to get rid of a problem, but this rarely works, because the problem is usually being caused by an unidentified situation within the organisation's underlying business processes.

Meanwhile the following Checklists cover the important aspects in summary form:

## Checklist: 10 rules of outsourcing

1. **Develop a strategy for outsourcing.** Outsourcing should always be measured against in-house solutions. This will help identify relative strengths and weaknesses for each alternative.

2. **Establish a rigorous provider selection process.** Check industry sources, existing clients, and financial health. Carefully analyse management depth, strategic direction, information technology capability, labour relations, and personal chemistry and compatibility.

3. **Clearly define your expectations.** Outsourcing relationships most often fail because of unrealistic expectations by companies that lack accurate or detailed knowledge about the volume, size and frequency of their shipments. Such inaccuracies result in arrangements that don't reflect reality.

4. **Develop a good contract.** Provide incentives to improve operations and productivity with both parties sharing the benefits. Clearly spell out obligations, expectations and remedies.

5.  **Establish sound policies and procedures.** In the ideal world, an operating manual will be developed jointly with the provider and contain all policies, procedures and other information necessary for the efficient operation of the outsourcing arrangement.

6.  **Identify and avoid potential friction points.** Both parties are usually aware of friction points that may arise. Develop a procedure for dealing with them in advance.

7.  **Communicate effectively with your logistics partner.** Poor communication is second only to poor planning as a cause of outsourcing relationship failure.

8.  **Measure performance, communicate results.** When setting up a relationship, clearly identify, agree upon and communicate standards of performance. Then measure performance regularly.

9.  **Motivate and reward providers.** Don't take good performance for granted. Compliments, recognition, awards, trophies and dinners are all proven motivators. Do whatever works for your particular circumstances, but do something.

10. **Be a good partner.** Good partnerships are mutually beneficial. Your logistics service provider's ability to serve you and your customers often can hinge on your own performance or lack thereof.

**Source:** Bob Trebilcock, Modern Materials Handling, 3/1/2004

# Checklist: 10 Questions before outsourcing logistics operations

1.  **Is logistics a non-core activity?** (Management control must however remain a core activity, as should, customer contact).

2.  **Can we release some capital?** (Third party industries have reported low ROCE ratios, typically 10 per cent).

3.  **Will we retain some operations in house?** (Maybe it will be useful to do this for cost comparisons and service benchmarking).

4.  **Will we retain Management expertise?** (Yes, very important, never sub contract control).

5.  **What increased monitoring will be needed?** (Should be the same as currently done, but especially watch customer service standards.

6.  **What are the risks of committing to one contractor?** (Flexibility in the contract maybe possible, alternatively, multi sourcing is the answer).

7.  **Will flexibility be increased?** (It should be flexible as in theory, the 3PL operator can maybe divert non-specialised resources elsewhere, and after all, transport and warehousing is their core business).

8.  **Will costs be reduced, whilst service increased?** (This is the ideal).

9.  **How will we account for future changes?** (The same as without the contractor presumably however it is the contract term and 'get outs' that is the issue here).

10. **Are there any The Transfer of Undertakings (Protection of Employment) Regulations (TUPE) legislation implications?** (Probably will not be if less than 5 people, if retain some control of say routing and if relocated. Probably will, if assets and or the whole business are transferred, however legal advice will be needed).

**Source:** Emmett, 2005, *Logistics Freight Transport*

# Checklist: Reported reasons for using 3PLs

- Customer satisfaction
- Financial benefit
- Speed, focus, and fire power
- Complex requirements with required flexibility
- Insufficient internal competence
- Need for unbiased expertise
- Capitalize on efficiencies
- Economic environment
- Economies of scale
- Planned/known/reduced costs
- Logistics is non-core
- ROCE as capital is released
- Asset utilisation improves
- Marginal size of operations
- Flexibility in 'spreading' peaks/troughs in delivery times and in future changes
- Use of better ICT
- Geographic specificities
- Management constraint
- Globalization

**Source:** Schneider Electric, Eye for Transport, 4th European 3PL Summit, Brussels October 2006.

# Pre-contract Award Management

This involves preparing a quality contract by considering the individual tasks required to be undertaken in the competitive tendering process and to the point of contract award.

The competitive tendering process includes the following standard procurement tasks, which need to be planned and considered against the need and requirements:

- Draft and agree the specification.
- Plan contract strategy.
- Agree evaluation criteria.
- Enquire and research the marketplace.
- Communicate with potential contractors.
- Possibly use a pre-qualification document to select tenderers.
- Request tenders and evaluate tenders.
- Tender negotiations.
- Recommend tender for award.
- Award contract.
- Debrief unsuccessful tenderers.

The methods used to draft and agree the specification, plan contract strategy, agree evaluation criteria, research the marketplace and communicate with potential contractors, are, amplified below, using in part the improvements model as follows:

distribution facility capacities and constraints; delivery cycle times; special customer or channel requirements; seasonality; procedures for returns, spares and service parts; hours of operation; and related factors.

This process has significant benefit by itself, even if no outsourcing ever results, as it can be the first time such a comprehensive picture has been put together. The answers provide for both an ongoing internal use and to also brief potential 3PL candidates in conjunction with the steps below.

### Know current levels costs and performance (where are we now?)
At some time there is a need to document the impacts of outsourcing logistics, for example:
* Have costs actually gone down?
* Is performance equivalent to or better, than what you had before?
* Are we getting our money's worth?

The only way to answer such questions is to have available the current baseline of cost and performance to enable the "before" in the "before-and-after" comparison.

Many organisations do not actually have a good view on their own cost and performance levels. For a shipment routing, it's not just the truck rate per mile/KM or the rate per 1000 kilos/CBM; what is affecting the performance are many reasons, for example, how much product was on the truck, how often was it delayed when loading /unloading, how frequently damage occurs, how fast the order was processed, how frequently backorders were involved, how much internal staff time was involved in fulfilling the customer requirements, etc.

3PLs also want and need this information so that they can evaluate what benefits they expect to provide and what goals they're expected to hit, as well as to what extent they will share in gains or losses as part of a performance-based contract.

### Develop the scope and objectives (where do we want to be)
It is critical to take the time to specify what is in scope and what is not and why. Does for example, transport management include all modes or just some; does it cover domestic or also international movements? Organisations need to clarify what they are trying to achieve through outsourcing, for example:

* Is it a reduction in costs?
* An improvement in service?
* A reduction in error rates?
* Shorter lead-times?
* Use of more advanced IT systems to plan and optimise operations?
* On-the-ground expertise in new markets?

Different objectives point to not only needing to have different directions in evaluating and selecting the logistics provider, but also to initially arrive at the clear and agreed SORs/specifications. A healthy debate on this subject is, therefore, beneficial.

What is needed here is to avoid a situation where potential 3PLs say something like "Thanks, but no thanks. You don't really know what you want, so we can't respond to you and won't participate in your selection process." It takes time and effort and cost to respond to requests so this is not an unusual situation. After all the 3PL view here is "If they do not know what they want, how can I give them something?"

Having clear objectives from the beginning also makes it much easier to evaluate the 3PL success later on. The following shows some of the wide-ranging evaluation criteria choices.

## Checklist: Criteria used to select a 3PL

- Market Intelligence
- Supply market and industry knowledge
- Market share the 3PL holds
- Background checks on the 3PL finance, equipment, facilities etc.
- RFQ Analysis
- Quality of the solution
- Customer focus
- Operations involvement vs. Sales pitch
- Ability to answer to terms and conditions
- Ability to optimize operations
- Clarity and measurability of the deliverables
- Certifications (sustainable development, security, quality, ethics, environment)
- ICT capabilities
- 3PL team background
- Proven track record
- Ability to become a key supplier or be a challenger
- Global reach
- Financial viability
- People
- Personal fit
- Willingness to engage in a long term relationship

Schneider Electric, Eye for Transport, 4th European 3PL Summit, Brussels October 2006.

**Build the right project team (how do we get there?)**
Logistics outsourcing of transport/warehousing can "knock on" and affect a wide range of activities such as manufacturing, purchasing, sales, customer service, finance, marketing, inventory, stock levels as well as the people involved. As already mentioned, it is therefore important from the beginning to involve each of these areas/departments. This is to establish requirements and objectives, which will also help in the later selection and assessment of the "best fit" 3PL.

To get the benefits of outsourcing, all of these activities/stakeholders have to go along with the results of the selection process, so it is best to involve them early, rather than announce an outcome that may then be resisted and thus doomed to failure. There are two simple steps to use here:

1. Firstly, appoint a dedicated project manager who "owns" the project and has clear responsibility for the identification and selection process and directing the activities of the team.

2. Secondly, have clear and visible top management commitment to set the tone, make resources available and break through the inevitable delays and blockages that occur. Not only do these factors help the project proceed more smoothly, they will improve the attention and responsiveness from 3PLs as they have a "one stop shop" as they can detect whether there is commitment and discipline to engage and work with them. They will then react accordingly.

Meanwhile **strategic issues** to be considered by top management involve considering, after the decision to contract to a 3PL contractor, then what for example:

- Will be our ability to change to another contractor or take back the operation in house?
- Are the internal implications?
- Are the risks involved?
- Will be our customer reactions, (customer contact must remain a core activity and should not be subcontracted)
- Will it assist in any internal change/new strategies/expansion?

## Checklist: "Extra" skills needed when managing 3PLs

- Analysis
- Change management
- Contract management
- Back-up plans
- Risk management
- Relationship handling
- 3PL Industry knowledge

Schneider Electric, Eye for Transport, 4th European 3PL Summit, Brussels October 2006.

**Which 3PL to contact (how do we get there?)**
There are literally hundreds of 3PLs and it is not possible to contact them all. Initial information gathering and informal meetings with logistics providers can be a good way to identify those 3PLs that have the promise of being a good match for you. Ask them, for example:

- What other customers have needs that are similar to ours?

- What is your experience with handling the unique and critical requirements of your organisation?
- What share of your customers is approximately similar to our organisation?
- How many of your other customers use the same combination of ICT, warehouse management and transportation systems that we have?
- What do you see as the keys to logistics success for organisations like us?

This involves being willing openly to share information about your situation and objectives. To effectively come up with a short-to-medium-size list of candidates, this requires asking some clear and direct questions early and guards against having only sessions with 3PLs that focus too much on high level 3PL corporate capability presentations such as "we are global, so here is a map that shows how global we are". Whilst such power point presentations may be useful, they can sometimes have a marketing/selling focus rather than one of factual telling, for example facts of the scale and size of such operations, people, equipments, owned facilities etc.

Starting with such early solid foundations means a smoother working towards satisfactorily completing the following standard procurement steps.

- Possibly use a pre-qualification document to select tenderers.
- Request tenders and evaluate tenders.
- Tender negotiations.
- Recommend tender for award.
- Award contract; and
- Debrief unsuccessful tenderers.

As has been shown there is much to be done in the pre-contract award management. Doing this correctly means that the wining contractor has been already involved and is already perhaps seen as being a part of the organisation. This is very important for the subsequent supplier management.

Regrettably, the formal adherence to rigid tender procedure policies can present a major barrier for some organisations. It is, therefore, perhaps no surprise that the subsequent award and contract does not then run smoothly. Those organisations that find they are unable to early share with potential suppliers must also *"...embark on a scheme of attitude and culture change, so that everyone with supplier contact, not just those in purchasing, understands the main implications of their behaviour and how their actions affect the way their suppliers respond and behave towards them".* (Supply Management 15 June 2000, Will Parsons).

## Post-Contract Award Management

After having made a fair and complete comparison, an award is made and the contract now needs managing.

The worst way to 'manage' a contract is simply to leave it take its course; it will, more than likely, go wrong and leave an incomplete audit trail. Let's be very clear here, control cannot be outsourced, and management control must remain a core activity. Effective contract management provides for the handling of contractual, commercial and collaboration aspects:

**1) Contractual:** Performance to a required standard and compliance with the contract conditions; for example, costs and services supplied are in accordance with the requirements of the contract and its terms and conditions. Contract control involves actively keeping the contractor's performance to the required standard. Participation by both parties is needed if this is to be successful, so that any problems can be quickly identified and resolved. It is therefore important that a sound working relationship is established.

If monitoring indicates that a contractor's performance has deteriorated, action will need to be taken. The nature of the action will depend upon the level of the under-performance or complaints. If regular monitoring is effectively carried out problems will be spotted early and the degree of any disruption from corrective action will be minimised. In most cases a discussion on the problem, will be all that is required to secure agreement on remedial action.

**2) Commercial:** Clear and documented records with evidence where necessary, to invoke any non-compliance procedures, for example, recording complaints received from customers of the service and recording customer satisfaction with the service. It is important for contract managers to have clear and documented evidence if contracts do not run smoothly. Records of all meeting and telephone conversations should be held on file. The contractor should be notified in writing of all instances of non-compliance, and a written timetable for rectification, should be drawn up. It is likely that the contractor will also be keeping records of the problems incurred with the contract.

If the contractor continually fails to perform, this may constitute a breach of contract. The severity of the failure and the cost to the organisation will need to be assessed. Legal advice may be required before any further action is considered. Below are examples of where default in a contract may arise from a failure to:

- Perform any part of the services.
- Provide financial or management information.
- Employ appropriately qualified, experienced, skilled or trained staff.
- Comply with legislation.
- Make payment to the 3PL on time (clearly both parties must fulfil their contractual obligations).

**3) Collaboration and relationships between the parties**, the way they regard each other and the way in which their relationship operates, is vital to making a success of the 3PL arrangement.

Although it is sometimes difficult to predict accurately where problems may arise, good contract management with regular dialogue between the contractor and customer will help to identify early, potential problems. This will enable problems to be dealt with swiftly and effectively and so prevent major disputes.

Active contract management therefore requires efficient two-way communications between both parties, which will anticipate problems, so that these are dealt with quickly and corrective action is taken to prevent similar problems from arising in future. This requires established lines of communication and an overall approach that will jointly and seamlessly manage and control change, for example making joint improvements

As identified by the OGC (2002), good contract management goes much further than ensuring that the agreed terms of the contract are being met – this is a vital step, but this contractual step is only the first of many. Whilst a successful relationship must involve the delivery of services that meet requirements, and the commercial arrangement must be acceptable to both parties (such as offering value for money for the customer and adequate profit for the provider), the collaboration between the parties, the way they regard each other and the way in which their relationship operates, is what is really critical in making a success of the arrangement.

No matter the scope or the terms of the contract, there will always be some tension between the different perspectives and perceptions of the customer/buyer and the supplier/ contractor. Contract management is about resolving such tension, and to do this, there must be an effective collaboration with the supplier/contractor that is based on mutual gains, understanding, trust and open communication.

**Control of change**
Contract requirements are often subject to change throughout the life of the contract. We live in a fast changing world with a future of "stable turbulence", and it is not, therefore, always possible to predict such changes and variations in advance or at the specification stage. It may be decided during the course of the contract, that a slight change to the requirements is needed.

Such changes to the requirements will often affect the cost and so will need to be recorded. Changes to the 3PL contract may also affect the following:

*   The initial specification can be now out of date.
*   The cost and service, for example, changed delivery times, locations.
*   The nature of the services being provided.

It will normally be the role of the contract manager to ensure that any need for any contract variation is recorded and the contract changed to be line with the newly agreed procurement procedures, where the variation, is clearly tied in with the main contract so that a clear audit trail is possible. Audit trails are especially important for those organisations in the public sector who find it essential to keep records of dealings with suppliers, whether written or verbal, as such records are required for:

*   Information if problems arise.
*   Reviewing meetings and re-negotiations.
*   Audit purposes.
*   Planning for any subsequent re-tendering processes.

**End of Contract/Completion Reports**
It is good practice at the completion of any contract to review and place on record what went well and what lessons can be learned for any future contracts, for example with a

Contractor Evaluation Report. The information on this report will be used to evaluate and monitor the effectiveness of the organisations contractors. This essentially covers the outcome and extent to which the expected benefits (deliverables) were achieved. Meanwhile, as a guide, acquiring industry knowledge of the 3PL industry performance can show the following:

## Checklist: European Logistics Service Providers End User Survey

Survey of 700 senior managers in hi-tech, automotive, consumer goods, pharmaceutical and retail sectors in UK, Benelux, France, Germany, Italy, Spain

3PLs have a weak performance in:
* Price
* Tailored solutions
* Reliability (the most important requirement)
* Customer service

3PLs would lose business if:
* Inferior value for money
* Lack of reliability
* Inferior service quality

Satisfied with 3PLs on:
* Expertise
* Size
* Geographical coverage

3PL "not a problem" areas are:
* Lack of geographical coverage
* Specific industry knowledge
* Limited service range

**Source:** SHD May 2004: Datamonitor "European Logistics Provider End User Survey".

**A Paradigm Change**
Through the 3PL decision, an organisation moves from a focus on protecting the "how" of business to managing the "what" of its business. This means changing the organisational structure from a focus of internal corporate competencies in the higher risk/strategically important zone to the external sourcing of lower risk/non-strategically important competencies. This requires a paradigm shift in the organisations management from being process operationally minded managers towards now being contract managers. The key attitudinal changes required as follows:

195

- **Respect the contractor.** Often, two different business cultures come together in a 3PL relationship, for example, the 3PL is contracted because they are "the experts" and the organisations staff must now present themselves professionally and acknowledge the 3PL's ability to do the work.
- **Develop Rapport.** A 3PL arrangement is an opportunity to move away from adversarial/transactional relationship to a collaborative/partnering supplier relationship. This requires the development of rapport between all of the key players.
- **Focus upon Project Milestones** (as already noted, project management is a good approach to 3PL management). Regular meetings are required to report on transition, optimization and process improvements. The 3PL must be regularly accountable but must also receive regular clear guidance.
- **Clear Statements of Deliverables.** There should be no doubt about the deliverables of the 3PL. They should be stated in the agreement but also clearly understood by the key players and regularly reviewed by them at an appropriate forum.
- **Staff Interaction.** Interaction is vital at both the management level and the working level. Contract management should always be on the lookout to facilitate interaction to head off potential problems and to encourage innovation and synergies.

Any eventual gap between planned and actual benefits of outsourcing logistics and the non achievement of the expected performance will not only be caused by the external 3PL; but also by internal barriers, such as resistance and failure to change attitudes. Consequently the required support to the new ways of working together has been stifled and prevented.

## Best Practice Contract Management

From the above look at 3PL contracts, we can identify the following aspects of good contract management. This can be summarised as follows:

1. **Good preparation.** An accurate assessment of needs/requirements helps to create a clear technical and/or performance based specification. Effective evaluation procedures and selection, against the specification of requirements, will then ensure that the contract is awarded to the right contractor.
2. **The right contract.** The contract is the legal foundation for the relationship. It should include aspects such as allocation of risk, the quality of service required, and value for money mechanisms, as well as procedures for communication and dispute resolution and the contractual obligations of the customer/contracting organisation.
3. **Empathy and understanding.** Each party needs to understand the objectives and business of the other. The customer must have clear business objectives, coupled with a clear understanding of what the contract will contribute to them; the 3PL contractor must also be able to achieve their objectives, including making a reasonable profit.
4. **Service delivery management and contract administration.** Effective governance will ensure that the customer gets what is agreed, to the level of quality required. The 3PL performance under the contract must be monitored to ensure that the customer continues to get what they expect.
5. **Collaboration and relationship management.** The eventual success of a contract depends on mutual trust and understanding, openness, and excellent

communications. These being just as important, (and may be more so), then the fulfilment of the legal terms and conditions.

6.  **Continuous improvement.** Improvements in price, quality or service should be sought and, where possible, built into the contract terms and the benefits shared.

7.  **People, skills and continuity.** There must be people with the right interpersonal and management skills to manage these relationships at all the multiple levels in the organisation. Clear roles and responsibilities should be defined, and continuity of key staff should be ensured as far as possible. A contract manager (or contract management team) should be designated early on in the procurement process.

8.  **Knowledge.** Those involved in managing the contract must understand the business fully and know the contract documentation inside out. This is essential if they are to understand the implications of problems or opportunities over the life of the contract.

9.  **Flexibility.** Management of contracts requires some flexibility on both sides and a willingness to adapt the terms of the contract to reflect a rapidly changing world. Problems are bound to arise that could not be foreseen when the contract was awarded.

10. **Change management.** Contracts should be capable of change (to terms, requirements and perhaps scope) and the relationship should be strong and flexible enough to facilitate it.

11. **Proactivity.** Good contract management is not reactive, but aims to anticipate and respond to business needs of the future.

# Supplier Management best practice

For reference purposes, the following is our summary of best practice:

1.  If a company does not have a basic supplier performance management process in place, it is very difficult to even start to think about supplier management. The first priority must be to know how key suppliers perform against the contract. Once the basics are in place then organisations can start to think about more sophisticated supplier management processes.

2.  Organisations must make sure that they prioritise and categorise carefully which suppliers to address, and we addressed this through the Kraljic procurement positioning tool techniques. Few organisations have the resources to carry out effective supplier management with a very large number of suppliers. It is far better to succeed with that important handful of suppliers first, and then, later, to grow the initiative.

3.  Organisations must be clear about the objectives of the supplier management process; they should clearly relate to the organisation's overall aims. For example, that might be working with the suppliers to achieve better value for money, or innovation or developing approaches to new markets. The supplier management programme must link clearly to the organisational key goals.

4.  It is important to recognise the mutuality of the relationship. Organisations must consider what the supplier wants out of the relationship and position their own objectives accordingly. A supplier management programme will only succeed with supplier co-operation; there must therefore be real mutual benefits.

5.  Organisations must be careful not to underestimate the resource needed to carry out supplier management effectively. As we saw, there are increasingly more involved levels of supplier development, which require additional resources to gain the additional benefits. Getting results needs detailed work with defined tools and processes, and mechanisms that may include joint working parties, detailed cost analysis, or combined development projects. Organisations must be prepared to allocate the pre-requisite resources into the process otherwise results will be disappointing.

6.  Data is important. Information must be regularly reviewed, shared and constructive feedback given. Organisations must have a clear view of their contractual relationship with their suppliers, including spend patterns and performance.

7.  Organisations must involve key internal stakeholders, supplier management cannot be a purely procurement department based activity. The cross-functional side of things is important and should dominate. Organisations need to ensure that everyone is really working to the agreed supplier management agenda.

8.  Organisations must consider who is best placed to handle different aspects of supplier management. For instance, there is the day-to-day collection of information in terms of the operational contract delivery, and there is the important aspect of managing the improvement over, for example, a two- to five-year development horizon with the supplier.

9.  Organisations can be creative; there are many different techniques, tools and processes that can be useful in this programme, such as secondments of key staff, brainstorming workshops, combined project teams and joint buyer/supplier conferences.

10.  Even your closest 'partner' may not meet your needs in the future, or they may decide to become a competitor, or withdraw from your business. Therefore, organisations must remember that relationships do not last forever and in parallel to supplier management, they also need to be thinking about alternative strategies, different suppliers and contingency plans.

# And Finally: Three Lessons from Experience

**1) Bill Knittle, Global Procurement Director, refining and marketing (R&M) BP:**
BP started its SRM programme in 2003 and Knittle says he has the "battle scars" to show for it.

First the company segmented its suppliers to decide where to concentrate its efforts. It examined assurance and compliance to check if it was getting what it should from current deals, looked at spend volume and the value of the deals it had in place, and also examined what suppliers thought. It did this with the help of Honda, Toyota and an independent survey.

"It was an eye-opener," Knittle says. Of BP's 51,000 suppliers, it discovered it had just six to eight key strategic vendors. The next tier, "sector-critical relationships", had around 170 suppliers, and there are another 800 with whom BP has sector and/or local relationships. It's SRM and supplier performance management programme - aimed at these groups - is expected to net savings of $200 million.

Start slowly with process-based decisions around supplier performance until trust is established, is his advice: "If you've been beating them up for the past few years it will take you at least 24 to 36 months to get them to talk about relationship management."

He said buyers had to send clear and consistent messages to suppliers and set KPIs appropriate to the relationship - for example, with top targets around innovation measurement for only your tier one suppliers. "Link your SRM to shareholder value (growth of business, cost efficiency, etc.) otherwise it's nice but it doesn't excite the senior manager. This has helped us."

A large number of things must be in place if an organisation is to make a success of SRM and, he suggests, those still working at a transactional level are not ready for it. KPIs should support the firm's overall objectives and performance management, clear strategic goals, the right contracts, effective planning and capable managers should all be in place: "Relationship management skills are a totally different skill-set. Don't expect anyone trained only to be aggressive for 20 years to be good at this," he adds.

**2) Joseph Youssef, Director of global technology supplier management, McDonald's:**
"Seventy-five percent of value can be lost if we don't do proactive SRM," says Joseph Youssef.

He believes executive sponsorship has been key to the success of SRM at McDonald's and says some of its suppliers have also appointed an executive sponsor to mirror the behaviour. "Conventional project sponsorship achieves only short-term goals. They need to invest a lot of time and effort." He says SRM helped the firm focus on long-term relationship needs and that it enhanced communication and helped to prevent "relationship value degradation". It also creates greater visibility, access to supplier capabilities and fosters innovation.

So what lessons has he learnt?
"Prioritise and focus. Don't think big picture idea, we tried it - it doesn't work, it failed miserably. Try one area, achieve it and move on. We started in IT, now we're moving into facilities and other areas and it's better that way.

"It's led to faster negotiations of additional services; tangible results have been achieved ($40 million a year contract over the past four years, $3.5 million savings in cost avoidance). It's also led to a better dialogue with suppliers. We didn't know what their pains were and what they needed. Now we have a better understanding of what they go through when we make demands on them."

**3) Paul Alexander, Head of Procurement, British Airways**
Alexander says the industrial action prompted by the dismissal of Gate Gourmet catering staff in 2005 made British Airways "think about upgrading SRM for the future".

In fact, he says, it is critical in an industry that has so many monopoly suppliers and is vulnerable to all manner of disruption - including weather, strikes and terrorism. "Playing suppliers off against each other is not the way of the future. It's a particular problem for airlines but it may also be a problem for you. You need to get the supplier to internalise you as the 'customer of choice'. We're moving into a world of scarcity, particularly because of the growth of India and China. My biggest challenge is competing with other buyers, not getting suppliers to compete."

Alexander says simple things such as writing thank-you letters have helped. "Even the language you use can drive a union between you and your suppliers. We say things like, 'What problem are we trying to solve?' Not too many suppliers are dependent on BA so this approach has been very successful."

**Source:** Supply Management 28 February 2008

# References

Aberdeen Group. 2006. *The Contract Management Report - Procurement Contracts.*

Aberdeen Group. 2007. *Sell Side Contract Management.*

Andersen & Gaute-Pettersen. 1996. *The Benchmarking Handbook.*

Arminas, D. 2004. "Supplier Relationships: Let's face the cost rises and advance", *Supply Management July 2004.*

Bagshaw, S. 2008. "BAE Systems: British Sea Power", *Supply Management, May 2008.*

Bailey, P., Farmer, D., Crocker, B., Jessop, D. and Jones, D. 2008. *Procurement Principles and Management.*

Baumber, C.S. 1993. "Benchmarking – Know Thy Self", BPICS Conference.

Birch, D. 2001. "Supplier Development: How do you do?" *Supply Management, March 2001.*

Bradley, A. 2005. "The Ups and Downs of Relationships", *Supply Management, October 2005.*

Brenchley, D. 2004. "Collaboration Made Easy", *Supply Management July 2004.*

Carr, A.A., Kaynak, H. 2007. "Communication methods, information sharing, supplier development and performance", *International Journal of Operations and Production Management, Vol 27 No 4.*

Checkett, S. 2008. "The CPO's Strategic Agenda", Aberdeen Group.

Clarke, E. 2006. "Evaluate to accumulate", *Supply Management, April 2006.*

Drucker, Peter. 2004. *The Daily Drucker.*

Doshi, B. 2004. "At the Controls", *Supply Management, November 2004.*

Ellinor, R. 2007. "SRM – Crowd Pleaser", *Supply Management, December 2007.*

Ellinor, R. 2008. "The A – Z of SRM", *Supply Management, February 2008.*

Ellinor, R . 2006. "Organisations find SRM hard to grasp", *Supply Management July 2006.*

Ellinor R,. 2005. "Study shows SRM Leaders", *Supply Management December 2005.*

Ellinor, R . 2006. "Carmakers SRM efforts start to pay off", *Supply Management June 2006.*

Ellison, H. 2003. "Supplier Management: Satisfaction Guaranteed", *Supplier Management, July 2003.*

Emmett, Stuart. 2005. *Logistics Freight Transport.* Cambridge Academic, Cambridge.

Emmett, Stuart. 2005. *Excellence in Warehouse Management.* John Wiley & Sons.

Emmett, Stuart. 2007. *The Relationship Driven Supply Chain*: a paper presented at the South African Production and Inventory Control Society SAPICS Conference, June 2007.

Emmett, Stuart. 2008. *Excellence in Supply Chain Management.* Cambridge Academic, Cambridge.

Emmett, Stuart. 2008. *Developing People Business Improvement Toolkit.* Management Books 2000 Ltd.

Emmett, S and Crocker, B. 2006. *The Relationship Driven Supply Chain.* Ashgate.

Emmett, S and Crocker, B. 2008. *Excellence in Procurement.* Cambridge Academic, Cambridge.

Emmett, S and Granville, D. 2007. *Excellence in Inventory Management.* Cambridge Academic, Cambridge.

Evans, P. 1998. "Supplier Certification: A starting point for business improvement", *BPICS Control, November 1998.*

Ford, I. 2003. "Supplier Management: Partners in Progress", *Supply Management, June 2003.*

Gilbert, H. 2006. "Great Expectations", *Supply Management June 2006.*

Hines, P., James and Jones. 1995. "The Supplier Development Matrix: A tool for awareness raising, acceptance and implementation planning", 2nd International Symposium on Logistics, July 1995, Nottingham.

Hull B. 2002. "A Structure for Supply Chain Information Flows and its application to the Alaskan crude oil supply chain." *Logistics Information Management, volume 15, number 1.*

Harvey Jones, John, Sir. 1995. *Altogether Now.* Random House.

*Human Resources,* June 2004.

Institute of Business Ethics (IBE). 2006. *Supplier Relationship* report.

John, G. 2005. "Purchasers not making the grade on policy or service", *Supply Management, May 2005.*

Johnson, R. 2003. "Supplier Management: A deal of time and effort", *Supply management April 2003.*

Kanter, J. 2008. "BMW looks to reduce lead-times and reduce costs", *Supply Management June 2008.*

Kanter, J. 2008. "Longer term deals are better than shorter contracts, says SM 100", *Supply Management, January 2008.*

Kanter, J. 2008. "Contracts: Laing O'Rourke cuts supply base", *Supply Management, March 2008.*

Kanter, J. 2008. "77% of purchasers keen to cut supplier numbers", *Supply Management, February 2008.*

Kaplan, R.S., Norton, D.P. 1996. *"The Balanced Scorecard: Translating Strategy into Action".*

Krause. D.R, Ellram, L.M. 1997. "Success Factors in Supplier Development", *International Journal of Physical Distribution & Logistics Management, Volume 27 No. 1, pp. 39-52.* MCB University Press.

Krause D.R. 1999. "The antecedents of buying organisation's efforts to improve suppliers", *Journal of Operations Management, Vol 17, No 2.*

Lamming, R., Harrison, D., Caldwell, N. 2000. "Transparency – Clearer Vision", *Supply Management, November 2000.*

*Logistics Manager* June, 2004.

Macbeth. D.K., Ferguson, N., Neil. G. 1993. *PSERG 2nd International Conference.*

Massey L., McCartney L. 1998. *"Managing Innovation with Suppliers",* 7th International IPSERA Conference, London.

Matthews, J. 2003. "Supplier Management: Why visiting pays", *Supply Management, 2003.*

Monczka R.M., Trent R.J., Callahan T.J. 1993. "Supply Base Strategies to maximise Supplier Performance", *International Journal of Physical Distribution and Logistics Management, Volume 23.*

Office of Government Commerce (OGC). 2002. *Contract Management Guidelines - principles for service contracts.*

Office of Government Commerce (OGC). 2006. *Supply Chain Management in Public Sector Procurement - a guide.*

Pearson, D. 1995. "Contractual Management of Risk". *Supply Management, November 2005.*

Philips Procurement Strategy. 1996. *European Procurement Materials Management.*

Polychronakis,Y.E., Syntetos, A.A. 2006. "Soft supplier management related issues: An empirical investigation", *International Journal of Production Economics 106.*

PTRM. 2007. *Global Supply Chain Trends 2008-2010.*

Reynolds A. 2006. "The Secrets of SRM", *Supply Management March 2006.*

Roberts, G. 2003. "Supplier Management A process of elimination", *Supply Management, June 2003.*

Sanchez-Rodriquez, C., Hemsworth, D., Martinez-Lorente, A.R. 2005. "The effect of supplier development initiatives on procurement performance: a structural model", *Supply Chain Management: An International Journal 10/4 289-301.* Emerald Group Publishing Ltd.

Sanchez-Rodriquez, C. and Hemsworth, D. 2005. "The effect of Supplier Development Initiatives on Procurement Performance: A Structural Model", *Supply Chain Management: An International Journal, Volume 10, No 4.*

Schneider Electric. 2006. *Eye for Transport* 4th European 3PL Summit, Brussels, October 2006.

Searles, R. 2003. "Supplier Management: The Goal Standard", *Supply Management, April 2003.*

Shaer, S.E. 2008. *"Skills Assessment Model" Project - BP Egypt.* CIPS Corporate Award.

Smith, P. 2005. "Supplier Relationship Management – More than a beautiful friendship", *Supply Management, February 2005.*

Snell, P. 2008. "Procurement to unlock expertise at Dairy Crest", *Supply Management January 2008.*

Snell, P. 2007. "Non-buyers can manage contracts", *Supply Management, October 2007.*

Snell, P. 2007. "Devolve contract management, buyers told", *Supply Management, October 2007.*

Snell, P. 2007. "Chrysler ups spend on low cost sourcing", *Supply Management, March 2007.*

Steele, P. and Court, B. 1996. *Profitable Purchasing Strategies.* McGraw-Hill Publishing Co.

Storage Handling & Distribution (SHD). 2004. Datamonitor *"European Logistics Provider End User Survey"*.

*The Sunday Times*, 11 February, 2007, and 16 March 2008.

"Supplier Co-ordination - Kyoryoku Kai". 2008. CIPS Positions on Practice, www.cips.org.

"Supplier Development". 2008. CIPS Positions on Practice, www.cips.org.

Supply Relationship Management, *Supply Management 28 February 2008*.

*Supply Management 15 June 2000*.

*Supply Management 18 January 2007*.

*Supply Management 28 February 2008*.

*Supply Management 13 March 2008:* "Flying in Formation" and "Barrett Homes repays £19k to supplier".

*Supply Management 27 March 2008*: "Power and Control".

*Supply Management 8 May 2008:* "Network Rail to improve its supplier relationships".

Thomas. A, and Barton. R,. 2007. "Integrating local suppliers in a global supply network", *Journal of Manufacturing Technology Management, Vol. 18 No.5, pp. 490-513*. Emerald Group Publishing Ltd.

Trebilcock, B. 2004. *Modern Materials Handling, 3 January 2004*.

*Toyota USA & Freight Provider Selection*; www.transportgistics.com.

Vail, S. 2006. "Man versus Machine", *Supply Management, May 2006*.

Waller, Alan, in Emmett and Crocker. 2006. *The Relationship Driven Supply Chain*. Ashgate.

# Index

Made in the USA
Lexington, KY
13 August 2010